Springer Series on Cultural Computing

More information about this series at http://www.springer.com/series/10481

Aaron Marcus · Masaaki Kurosu
Xiaojuan Ma · Ayako Hashizume

Cuteness Engineering

Designing Adorable Products and Services

 Springer

Aaron Marcus
Aaron Marcus and Associates
Berkeley, CA
USA

Masaaki Kurosu
The Open University of Japan
Tokyo
Japan

Xiaojuan Ma
Department of Computer Science
 and Engineering
The Hong Kong University of Science
 and Technology
Kowloon
Hong Kong

Ayako Hashizume
Tokyo Metropolitan University
Tokyo
Japan

ISSN 2195-9056   ISSN 2195-9064   (electronic)
Springer Series on Cultural Computing
ISBN 978-3-319-87200-1   ISBN 978-3-319-61961-3   (eBook)
DOI 10.1007/978-3-319-61961-3

Printed on acid-free paper

This Springer imprint is published by Springer Nature
The registered company is Springer International Publishing AG
The registered company address is: Gewerbestrasse 11, 6330 Cham, Switzerland

Foreword

Design has always evolved by reflecting new cultural and technological paradigms in design methods and processes. In the past Machine Age, design put focus on "comfortable design" to fit mechanical properties to people's physical characteristics like anthropometry or strength. Likewise, as computers began to support human cognition and information processing, user-interface design or interaction design has become a major design challenge to support users' cognitive characteristics. Now once again, we are on the verge of a new technological paradigm, which supports emotion. Products are beginning not only to perform commands given by users, but also to tell their opinions and even cheer up depressed human beings. People increasingly are spending more time in doing non-tasks like unconscious and purposeless interactions with mobile phones, for which usability, user-experience, and user-centeredness no longer suffice alone to provide solutions. In the past few years, user-centered design methods have been criticized for being too deterministic, a closed system, and for ignoring use-time. So we have moved on. Welcome to the age of artificial intelligence (AI) and robots. Yet, are we really ready for welcoming fully this new age? We might not have much of a choice. As Patrick Whitney argued at the dawn of the information age, "*it will be up to us to determine our role in this new age. If we do not, others will. Our alternative is our own obsolescence. Industrial designers, in particular, could soon be remembered with the same affectionate nostalgia as blacksmiths and Linotype men.*"

The theme of this book, cuteness, has its significant meaning in that it can shed some light on the challenges given us by this new age. Nowadays, we are beginning to interact with products using the same voice we human beings use to communicate with each other. Products are no longer limited to passively performing commands given by a user and instead proactively talk to us first. If this way of human-to-human-like communication becomes more sophisticated and broadly accepted, wouldn't it be consequential for us designers to start defining the personality of a product and design specific product characters? We might as well create a new discipline of *personality design*. If so, the study of "cuteness" would certainly be a good way to open up "personality design," because "cute": is indeed one of the most frequently used words for describing personality. However, language is one of the most culture-sensitive elements, and the contextual meaning of cuteness differs from culture to culture. For example, the Japanese equivalent of cute, *kawaii*, has higher contextual meaning than the English "Cute." This book shows great value in making us think about these details.

Perhaps the greatest value of this book is to provide readers with a theoretical framework and model for understanding personality attributes like "elegant" or "sophisticated" rather than simple definitions and cultural perspectives regarding cuteness itself. Furthermore, this theoretical framework can be applied to describe and design the personality of future AI products to come, as AI technology may soon reach sophistication levels of human-to-human communication.

This book opens new horizons and accomplishes this innovation even without having any solid or well-established body-of-knowledge. Thus, this type of pioneering book, with its cutting-edge theme, makes a significant contribution by provoking critical questions rather than generating a particular solution. Since the contributing authors have very diverse backgrounds, this book considerably broadens the scope of studying cuteness and discovers new issues by exposing the differences between different perspectives rather than creating one specific unified theory. The coauthors of this book, Aaron Marcus, Masaaki Kurosu, Xiaojuan Ma, and Ayako Hashizume, creatively differ from each other; however, they are on the same boat in their enthusiasm for the study of new field. Someone once said that "a subject important enough to warrant a large book should be introduced by a small one." Certainly the study of cuteness deserves a thick book, but I hope this one here before us can stand as such a small and "cute" one.

Seoul, South Korea   Kun-Pyo Lee

Preface

One might say that the origins of this book go back many decades, to when I was first motivated to draw Walt Disney cartoon characters as a child of about 8. Shortly afterward, I visited Disney Land for the first time in about 1957, 2 years after the theme park opened in 1955. I was very moved by and interested in Mickey Mouse, among other characters. I read and collected thousands of comic books as a teenager.

Many decades later in 1990, I drew chapter-opening cartoons for my first book, *Human Factors and Typography for More Readable Programs* (Baecker and Marcus 1990), coauthored with Prof. Ron Baecker, University of Toronto. In 1991, writing user Interfaces for the 90s with Prof. Andries van Dam, (van Dam and Marcus 1991), I began to show user interfaces that were designed for particular cultures, ages, and genders. In 1999, I began to study user-interface design across cultures and published several articles about this topic. After my first tour of China in 2002, I began to pay more attention to the growing number of cute forms in products, advertisements, movies, and other forms of communication. I wrote about the "Cult of Cute" in an essay for my "Fast Forward" column in ACM SIGCHI member-publication's *Interactions* magazine that year (Marcus 2002).

After years photographing cute forms in China, Japan, South Korea, in countries of Europe, in the USA, in South Africa, and elsewhere, in 2014, while attending the International Design and Human Factors Conference organized by Prof. Ren Xiangshi at the Kochi University of Technology, to give a keynote lecture for the conference, I was fortunate to meet Ma Xiaojuan, then with Huawei and later at the University of Science and Technology in Hong Kong. I was delighted to discover that she, too, was interested in all of the cute characters, images, and products that could be found in many countries like China and Japan. We spent an afternoon and part of several evenings photographing many examples. We discussed the possibility of writing an article about cuteness, especially in relation to China, and we were able to publish a paper in the *Proceedings* of the conference that I chair, Design, User-Experience, and Usability 2016 (Marcus and Ma 2016). For the paper, we began an initial taxonomy of cuteness, which seemed more complex than I had ever previously imagined. We also came to realize how many examples we had collected on this topic, how more and more computer-based imagery employed cute forms, and how complex the subject matter seemed, especially in relation to the history of cuteness in East Asian countries, about which I knew relatively little at the time.

Prof. Ma and I began to outline a book-length treatment of the topic. I was fortunate to benefit from her insights and to learn that Prof. Masaaki Kurosu and Prof. Ayako Hashizume were interested and available to assist us, providing valuable insights from a Japanese perspective. Through them, we were able to convince Sanrio to permit us to interview the managing designer of Hello Kitty. Through my own contacts with Mr. Wang Wentao, a noted user-experience designer at Baidu, we also were able to secure an interview with him that provided a Chinese perspective.

Our resultant book provides a start at analyzing what cuteness is and how it can be used to design products and services, especially for computer-based media. Commercial examples of the use of cuteness are appearing more and more in products and services of all kinds, especially in communication and entertainment media. We have extended our taxonomy and provided access to designers thinking about incorporating cuteness.

I am grateful for the cooperation and contributions of my coauthors and to all those who provided time, thoughtful insight, and assistance to us incompleting this book. We hope that readers find this book usable, useful, and appealing.

Berkeley, CA, USA   Aaron Marcus
June 2017

References

Baecker R, Marcus A (1990) Human factors and typography for more readable programs. Addison-Wesley, Reading, MA

Marcus A (2002) The cult of cute: the challenge of user-experience design. Interactions 9(6): 29–34. doi:10.1145/581951.581966

Marcus A, Ma X (2016) Cuteness design: an initial analysis. Proc. Design, User Experience, and Usability Conference, Toronto, 17–22 July 2016. In: HCII 2016 Proc. London: Springer. http://2016.hci.international/proceedings

van Dam A, Marcus A (1991) User-interface developments for the nineties. Computer 24(9): 49–57

Acknowledgements

The authors acknowledge (Baidu UX Dept, 2014), which stimulated some of the original discussions for this book. The authors also acknowledge two previous papers that formed a basis for this Chap. 1: Marcus and Baradit (2015) and Marcus and Ma (2016).

The authors also acknowledge the assistance of Ms. Yuko Yamaguchi and Ms. Kyoko Obata of Sanrio, and Mr. Wentao Wang of Baidu, who made time available to complete the interviews in Chaps. 5 (Japan) and 6 (China).

The authors additionally acknowledge the patience and encouragement of Ms. Helen Desmond, Editor, Springer UK, during the many months of preparation of this book.

Contents

1 Introduction 1
  1.1   History of Cuteness 1
  1.2   Definition of Cuteness 8
  1.3   Cuteness Issues 9
  1.4   User-Centered Design and Cuteness 9
  1.5   Market Research and Cuteness 13
  1.6   Internationalization, Globalization, Cross-Cultural User-
         Experience Design, and Cuteness 14
  1.7   Personas and Cuteness 20
  1.8   Use Scenarios and Cuteness 20
  1.9   Persuasion Theory and Cuteness 22
  1.10 Metaphor Design and Cuteness 23
  1.11 Information Architecture Design (Mental Model and
         Navigation) and Cuteness 24
  1.12 Look-and-Feel Design (Appearance and Interaction)
         and Cuteness 24
  1.13 Cuteness Guidelines 25
  1.14 Examples of Cuteness in UX of Computer-Based
         Products/Services 26
  1.15 Concluding Comments 27
  References 28

2 Cuteness in Japan 33
  2.1   Cuteness and *Kawaii* 33
       2.1.1   "*Kawaii*" as a Translation of "Cute" 33
       2.1.2   The Word "Cute" 33
       2.1.3   "*Kawaii*" Without the Meaning of Acuteness 34
       2.1.4   "*Kawaii*" and its Derivatives 35

2.2   Historical Overview of *Kawaii* in Japan   35
       2.2.1   *Heian* Era (794–1185)   35
       2.2.2   After *Heian* Era and *Edo* Era (1603–1868)   38
       2.2.3   *Meiji* Era (1868–1912) and *Taisho* Era (1912–1926)   39
       2.2.4   *Showa* Era (1926–1989)   40
2.3   The Popularity of *Kawaii*   40
       2.3.1   *Kawaii* is Now Flooding Japan   40
       2.3.2   *Kawaii* is also Trending in the World   41
2.4   Three Types of *Kawaii*   42
       2.4.1   Psycho-physical *Kawaii*   43
       2.4.2   Cultural *Kawaii*   44
       2.4.3   Generic *Kawaii*   49
       2.4.4   Other Types of *Kawaii*   51
2.5   *Kawaii* Culture Today   55
       2.5.1   Related Concepts   55
       2.5.2   Desire to be *Kawaii*   56
       2.5.3   *Kawaii* and Beautiful   56
       2.5.4   *Kawaii* and Horror   59
2.6   Conclusion   60
References   60

3   **Cuteness in China**   63
    3.1   Evolution of the Meaning of Cuteness in Chinese Literature   63
    3.2   Evolution of the Perception of Cuteness in Chinese Culture   64
           3.2.1   Lovely in Traditional Chinese Culture   64
           3.2.2   *Kawaii* Culture   65
           3.2.3   *Moe* Culture   66
           3.2.4   *Baozou* (Rage) Comic Phenomenon   67
    3.3   Cuteness Industry in China   78
           3.3.1   Conventional Culture Industry   80
           3.3.2   Internet Technology Industry   81
           3.3.3   From Original ACG IP to User-Centric IT:
                   A Case Study of How Cuteness Bridges Culture
                   and Technology in China   81
    3.4   Summary   89
    References   90

4   **Taxonomy of Cuteness**   93
    4.1   Styles of Cuteness   93
    4.2   Strategies of Playing Cute   115
    4.3   Higher Level Taxonomical Features of Cuteness   116
    4.4   Conclusions   118
    References   118

5 Interview with Yuko Yamaguchi (Hello Kitty Designer) 119
   5.1   Introduction 119

**6 Cuteness Design: Interview with Wentao Wang, Senior
User-Experience Designer, Baidu, Beijing, China** 147
   6.1   Introduction 147
   6.2   Background/Personal Questions 147
   6.3   Cuteness-Related Questions 149
   6.4   Sociocultural Differences-Related Questions................ 150

7 Conclusions 155

Index 157

About the Authors

Aaron Marcus Principal of Aaron Marcus and Associates (AM+A), and Editor-in-Chief *Emeritus* of *User-Experience* Magazine, is a pioneer of user-experience design, publisher of 29 books and more than 300 articles, and the first graphic designer to be elected to both the CHI Academy and to the AIGA Fellows. AM+A has been in business for more than 35 years, providing user-centered solutions on projects ranging from start-up ventures to business applications launched by some of the largest companies in the world. AM+A has served approximately 300 clients and completed approximately 500 projects.

Masaaki Kurosu is Professor *Emeritus* at the Open University of Japan, since 2017 and is an *Emeritus* President of HCD-Net after working as a President for 10 years. He was a professor at the Open University of Japan for 2009–2017 and was a professor at NIME for 2001–2009, a professor at Shizuoka University for 1996–2001. He was formerly working for Hitachi Ltd. at the Design Center and the Central Research Laboratory for 1978–1996. He proposed the concept of User Engineering, AET (Artifact Evolution Theory), ERM (Experience Recollection Method), and other usability/UX-related methods and concepts.

Xiaojuan Ma is Assistant Professor of the Human–Computer Interaction Initiative in the Department of Computer Science and Engineering at the Hong Kong University of Science and Technology. She received her Ph.D. degree in Computer Science at Princeton University. Before joining HKUST, she was a post-doc at the Human–Computer Interaction Institute of Carnegie Mellon University, a research fellow in the National University of Singapore, and a researcher at Huawei Noah's Ark Lab. Her background is in Human–Computer Interaction. She is particularly interested in multimodal affective computing in the domain of ubiquitous, social, and crowd computing and Human–Robot Interaction.

Ayako Hashizume is Assistant Professor at the Tokyo Metropolitan University since 2012. Her research interests include psychology of emotion and *kansei*, engineering in relation to Human-Centered Design and UX (user-experience). She was awarded the kids design prospective competition 2008 from the Japan Kids Design Association, the best design prize at the design marathon 2009 from the International Association for Universal Design, and the research prize 2013 from the Funai Foundation for Information Technology. She is a Chief of the SIG-*kansei* of HCD-Net. She received her Ph.D. in *kansei* Science from Tsukuba University, Japan, in 2011.

Chapter 1
Introduction

1.1 History of Cuteness

In our own lives, many of us have enjoyed playing as children with cute teddy bears, dolls, and/or other toys. When we began to read a language, illustrated stories often depicted cute, cuddly animals, people, and objects. Many people probably think they have a reasonably stable, inclusive understanding of what is cute, and what is not.

What about previous generations? What about previous millennia? Did prehistoric people produce cute artifacts? Did ancient civilizations in Central/South America, Europe, Africa, the Middle East, India, and East Asia produce cute artifacts from earliest times? What about other countries today, and other cultures? How did cuteness arise? Is it hardwired into our genetics, bodies, and minds? To discuss all of these issues completely would be a lengthy, complex narrative beyond the scope of this volume. We shall look at a more limited scope, especially in relation to computer-based products and services.

The origins of cuteness seem a little ambiguous. In some cases, we may ascribe today some qualities of cuteness to ancient cult objects like fertility symbols or game-piece tokens, *e.g.*, the abstract simplicity of Greek Cycladic art (see Fig. 1.1).

Another example is the use of small hands at the ends of rays streaming from the sun's image that appear on a stele carved to celebrate the sun deity with its representative on earth, the Pharaoh Akhenaten (who ruled about 1353–1336 BCE in the 18th Dynasty of Egypt), and his wife Nefertiti (see for example: https://ancientneareast.org/2014/01/03/the-enigma-of-akhenaten/). We might consider these hands cartoon-like and cute. The ancient Egyptians probably did not. It seems that some cultures/times may consider artifacts of another culture and/or distant time to be cute, which people of that other culture/time might not, and vice versa.

When did the "modern" concept of cuteness arise?

As Boyle and Kao (2016) note in a call for contributions to *The Retro-Futurism of Cuteness*, "the *OED* dates the first reference to "cute" in the sense of 'attractive,

© Springer International Publishing AG 2017
A. Marcus et al., *Cuteness Engineering*, Springer Series on Cultural Computing,
DOI 10.1007/978-3-319-61961-3_1

Fig. 1.1 Drawing of a typical ancient Greek Cycladic art (head of the figure of a woman) drawn by co-author Marcus as a composite from three images of artifacts made approximately 4500 years ago (2700–2500 BCE). See for example: http://www. metmuseum.org/toah/works-of-art/64.246/. Drawing by Aaron Marcus, used with permission

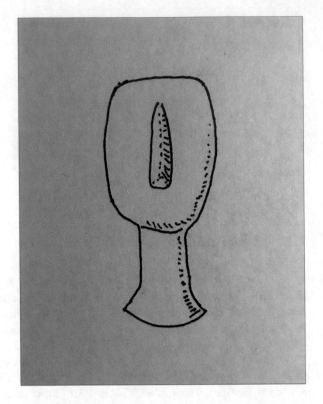

pretty, charming' to 1834. In 2005 and 2012, Sianne Ngai, channeling [the artists] Takashi Murakami and Andy Warhol, offered a critical overview of the cuteness of the twentieth-century *avant-garde*."

One may well ask if there were classical, medieval, Renaissance, Victorian, and other earlier forms, or styles, of cuteness, just as there are in painting, architecture, music, *etc.* Certainly there were theories of "beauty" or "aesthetics" in ancient Western and Eastern schools of thought that sought to define aesthetics in general, ideal proportions, harmonious colors, and desirable relationships among parts. One can mention the works of Aristotle in Europe, Confucius in China, and Bharata Muni in India. Yet cuteness often features forms, sizes, angles, curves, and components that are not typical of classical, or even modern, forms of aesthetic "correctness."

Boyle and Kao put it well: "Cuteness is neither the sublime nor the well-proportioned. It is a bastard child of the dainty and the dumpy; what's beautiful may not be cute, but what's ugly and monstrous may be. Cute cues and affects: softness, roundness, infancy, femininity, helplessness, vulnerability, harmlessness, play, enjoyment, awkwardness, neediness, intimacy, homeliness, and simplicity. At the same time, cuteness is cheapness, manipulation, delay, repetition, hierarchy, immaturity, frivolity, refusal, tantrum, and dependence. Cuteness is perhaps *the* aesthetic threshold: '*too* cute' is a backhanded compliment. And more than the pop cultural *kawaii* (literally, 'acceptable love'), 'cute'—the aphetic [shortened] form of 'acute'—also carries the sense of 'clever, keen-witted, sharp.' The Latin *acutus* embraces the sharpened, the pointed, the nimble, the discriminating, and the piercing. To be cute is to be in pain. Cuteness is therefore a figure of Roland Barthes's *punctum* or Georges Bataille's point of ecstasy."

For many decades in the twentieth and twenty-first centuries, cute toys, animations, publications, and images have circulated among many cultures. They are often associated with and used widely in products/services for children. In fact, cuteness often, but not exclusively seems to use childlike features (in human beings or animals, for example): large eyes, big heads, large foreheads, diminished arms and legs, but enlarged feet or hands, the very proportions of many babies.

Some analysts attribute cuteness to a protective inducement to caregiving to babies. One citation appears in the Wikipedia entry for cuteness (see https://en.wikipedia.org/wiki/Cuteness, viewed on December 6, 2016.) regarding the biological function of cuteness:

"Konrad Lorenz argued in 1949 that infantile features triggered nurturing responses in adults and that this was an evolutionary adaptation which helped ensure that adults cared for their children, ultimately securing the survival of the species. Some later scientific studies have provided further evidence for Lorenz's theory. For example, it has been shown that human adults react positively to infants who are stereotypically cute. Studies have also shown that responses to cuteness—and to facial attractiveness in general—seem to be similar across and within cultures" (referencing Van Duuren et al. 2003). In a study conducted by Stephan Hamann of Emory University, he found using an fMRI, that cute pictures increased brain activity in the orbital frontal cortex (Schneider 2013).

Also consider gender differences. The following three paragraphs are cited, as before, from https://en.wikipedia.org/wiki/Cuteness, viewed on December 6, 2016:

"Gender differences: The perceived cuteness of an infant is influenced by the gender and behavior of the infant (Koyama et al. 2006; Karraker and Stern 1990). In the Koyama, et al. research, female infants are seen as cute for the physical attraction that female infants display more than male infants; whereas research by Karraker and Stern demonstrates that a caregiver's attention and involvement in the male infant's protection could be solely based on the perception of happiness and attractiveness of the child".

"The gender of an observer can determine their perception of the difference in cuteness. In a study by Sprengelmeyer et al. (2009) it was suggested that women were more sensitive to small differences in cuteness than the same aged men. This suggests that reproductive hormones in women are important for determining cuteness".

"This finding has also been demonstrated in a study conducted by Alley (1981), in which he had 25 undergraduate students (consisting of 7 men and 18 women) rate cuteness of infants depending on different characteristics such as age, behavioral traits, and physical characteristics such as head shape, and facial feature configuration".

Consider one modern example: Mickey Mouse. At one point in time, Walt Disney's Mickey Mouse character, introduced in 1928, became one of, or *the*, most widely known image/character in the world, surpassing even images of Santa Claus. Suddath (2008) outlines the historical development of the Mickey Mouse character and its change of visual appearance, from a less appealing rodent in his first visualizations, with long nose and narrow face, to the big-eyed round-faced, circular-eared icon of the present day. The Disney Corporation in some usages has reduced the Mickey Mouse form to simply three intersecting circular disks, a larger one for the head and two smaller ones for the ears. This "evolution" is summarized symbolically in the accompanying Fig. 1.2.

In the past few decades, cute products/services, images, icons, *etc.*, have appeared extensively in East Asian countries (China, Japan, South Korea, Taiwan, in particular). The role and characteristics of cuteness in Asia are worthy of separate consideration, and are discussed later. In part, the increased use of cuteness in East Asian countries may stem from the popularity of *animé*, comics, and electronic games, the audiences for which are no longer limited to children, teenagers, and young adults.

Cuteness has been used to define and brand computer-based products/services (*e.g.,* the MIUI themes of recent Xiaomi phones in China), or the cat in Alibaba's shopping screen (Fig. 1.3). While cuteness seemingly has less impact in Africa, Europe, India, South America, and even the US, the globalization of products/services (*e.g.,* the Hello Kitty brand from Sanrio, Line, and Wechat) coming from East Asian countries makes it likely that cuteness will be incorporated

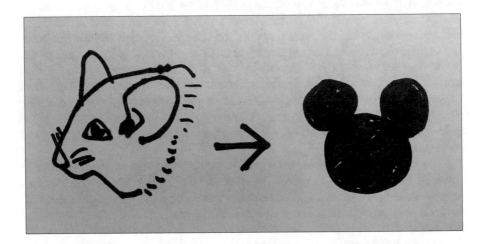

Fig. 1.2 Symbolic evolution of the Mickey Mouse character since its introduction. The Mickey Mouse cartoon character is an amusing, popular creature and the official mascot of The Walt Disney Company. Walt Disney and Ub Iwerks at the Walt Disney Studios in California created Mickey Mouse in 1928. The character's transformation over the past nine decades seems to give him more baby-like characteristics, making him more appealing (cartoon image by Aaron Marcus and used with permission)

Fig. 1.3 Example of Chinese cuteness found throughout cities, publications, Websites, and applications: typical double 11 shopping festival screen showing cute contents. (*Image Source* Tmall.com, Copyright 2015, used with permission)

more and more into many products/services, their devices, user interfaces, and branding.

An example is the extensive use of emoticons in the Japanese Line application and the Chinese WeChat application. Now, even Skype, which was founded in 2003 by Swedish and Danish persons with Skype software from Estonia, and which is now owned by Microsoft in the US, has featured cute icons (Fig. 1.4), some of which seem culturally centered for a particular country (images of a Turkey for US Thanksgiving Day). Recently Skype introduced, as have its competitor messaging and communication applications, an extensive collection of animated cute cartoon mini-segments complete with music and sound.

All of these products/services comprise user-experiences (UXs), that is, user interfaces, user touch points, *etc.*, which must be usable, useful, and appealing, and which can meet the needs/preferences of major stakeholders (the user community, engineering, marketing, business management, government, investors, and journalists). We believe cuteness can contribute to the success of a product/service's user-experience success by increasing appeal and memorability, and by helping to clarify concepts. Cuteness may contribute independently to the success of a product's or a service's branding by becoming specifically desired by current or future customers. There is consequently a challenge to create successful UXs that are functional, but also cute in form. Exploring UX cuteness can cover country/culture criteria, design philosophy, methods, evaluation criteria for stakeholders, and relations among stakeholders.

Computer-based (especially mobile and consumer-oriented) products/services are produced/consumed worldwide. Designers/developers must be aware of culture differences in thinking about cute UX designs, even for diverse domestic markets. The focus on cuteness seems especially important for Asian cultures, which give increased attention to aesthetic appeal and fun in the UX in comparison to Western

Fig. 1.4 Examples of cute emoticons (some culturally oriented in Skype), including a dancing turkey for use during the Thanksgiving (US) holiday. More recent images (May 2017), include dynamic, visually complex, animated emoticons, with photographs, videos SkypeMojis (TM), music, voices, and other multimedia characteristics (images © Copyright 2017 by Skype and used with permission from Skype Communications S.a.r.l)

Dancing Thanksgiving turkey   (turkey)

Hug   (hug)

cultures (Frandsen-Thorlacius et al. 2009). Cuteness engineering or design, culture theory, and design theory in relation to applying cuteness to products/services in many different cultures and contexts are all interconnected. Culture theories and models and user-centered design theory can serve as a basis for analyzing cuteness in mobile devices, publications, and Websites, for example. Cuteness can be connected to time orientation, spatial relations, family structure, gender roles, beauty, happiness, health, money/wealth, age/aging, groups/individuals, privacy/security, trust, and persuasion/behavior change.

In this introduction, we shall have an opportunity to comment on cuteness in relation to personas, use scenarios, information architecture (metaphors, mental models, and navigation), and look-and-feel (appearance and interaction) for products/services. As well, we shall consider Asian factors, especially in China, because of the growing impact of the Chinese marketplace.

Fig. 1.4 (continued)

1.2   Definition of Cuteness

As stated earlier in Marcus and Ma (2016) and edited here slightly, we propose a simplified definition of cuteness: "a characteristic of a product, person, thing, or context that makes it appealing, charming, funny, desirable, often endearing, memorable, and/or (usually) non-threatening. Cuteness as a concept is nuanced and complex."

One recent etymological essay of "cute" by Katy Waldman in *Slate* (Waldman 2015) notes the following:

"Cute's history argues for leniency. When the word first appeared in English in 1731, it was a shortened form of acute, the adjective meaning "shrewd," "keen," or "clever." It even had its own opening apostrophe—'cute'—to let you know it had been clipped. (Whether all abbreviations are somewhat cute, as in "heartwarmingly diminutive," is a question for minds cuter, as in "more cunning," than mine.) A "cute remark" back in Victorian England was a quick-witted one. So was the "cute man" in Dickens' 1841 book Barnaby Rudge. And so was a cute girl. In 1882, the Manchester Evening Mail ran a piece defending the typical American young woman as being just "as cute as the masculine Yankee," by which it meant she was equally sharp and spirited."

And further.

"You can thank American school kids for the more familiar "attractive," "pretty," or "charming" evolution of the term. This confusion of physical and mental appreciation—from the shapeliness or comeliness of a line of thinking to the elegant cut on a garment—misled my friend, who wanted to praise an argument on its brainy merits, into dinging it as trivial and superficial. Once cute's slang meaning caught on in the mid 1830s, it was used to describe, among other things, small socks, a nice, orderly study room, the narrow and beautiful vasculature of old city streets, and "a French accent … reminiscent of the naughty–naughty twitterings of a Parisian miss on the English musical comedy stage." Maybe that same bus that shuttles the modifier "smart" between ideas and outfits helped cute migrate from an intellectual value system to an aesthetic one.

"But in those early examples—the socks, the alleys, the young Parisian—yet another transformation is taking place. The smartness or "just-so"-ness of cute is also manifesting in the size of the noun being modified. In 1941, for instance, Aldous Huxley wrote of a "tiny boy … looking almost indecently cute in his claret-colored doublet and starched ruff.' I'm reminded of how Marianne Moore's poetic ideal—'neatness of finish'—was occasionally misread as a sign of the smallness, the modesty, of her ambitions. Something about being neat and appropriate apparently translates into being tiny: There's a sense of containment and easy comprehension. By the time Boyz II Men were singing about their "cutie pie" and websites devoted to 'cute little kittens' were springing up, cute had become a receptacle for all these related ideas: aesthetic charm, minuteness, childhood, femininity—with a lingering hint of wiliness thrown in for good measure."

1.3 Cuteness Issues

We believe it important to consider several issues of cuteness engineering, or cuteness design, in UX design:

- What is the taxonomy of cuteness?
- Where has cuteness been used in computer-based products/services?
- How does cuteness work or become effective?
- What guidelines exist for cuteness design?
- What information resources exist for the cuteness designer?
- How can local developers create successful cuteness user-experience for domestic and foreign products and services?
- How can foreign software/hardware developers create a successful user-experience for products and services in other countries/cultures?
- Is there a significant difference in Asian (*e.g.*, Chinese cuteness), as opposed to Western cuteness?
- What is the nature of the cuteness in China, Japan, South Korea, and/or Japan? What are the similarities and differences?
- Are there any significant design patterns for cuteness in different specific contexts, or across all contexts?
- How does cuteness change over time? What are the characteristics of these changes? Is there an acceleration of the speed of change in the last 30 years?

We explore a number of these issues and base our hypothesis of emerging cuteness design on examination of hundreds of images gathered over 10 years by coauthor Marcus and 5 years by coauthor Ma, and by previous qualitative and quantitative research. We hope to raise usable, useful, and appealing issues that may stimulate thinking and research among many professions and academic disciplines concerned with "pure" and "applied" cuteness engineering/design.

1.4 User-Centered Design and Cuteness

As discussed in many books and publications, *e.g.*, Marcus (2015a, b) and Hartson and Pyla (2012), user-centered design (UCD) links the process of developing software, hardware, the user interface (UI), and the total user-experience (UX) to the people who will use a product/service. The user-experience can be defined as the "totality of the [...] effects felt by a user as a result of interaction with, and the usage context of, a system, device, or product, including the influence of usability, usefulness, and emotional impact during interaction, and savoring the memory after interaction" (Hartson and Pyla 2012). That definition means the UX goes well beyond usability issues, involving, also, social and cultural interaction, value-sensitive design, emotional impact, fun, and aesthetics.

The UCD process focuses on users throughout all these development steps, or tasks, which sometimes occur iteratively:

- Plan: Determine strategy, tactics, likely markets, stakeholders, platforms, tools, and processes.
- Research: Gather and examine relevant documents, stakeholder statements.
- Analyze: Identify the target market, typical users of the product, personas (characteristic users), use scenarios, competitive products.
- Design: Determine general and specific design solutions, from simple concept maps, information architecture (conceptual structure or metaphors, mental models, and navigation), wireframes, look and feel (appearance and interaction details), screen sketches, and detailed screens and prototypes.
- Implement: Script or code specific working prototypes or partial so-called "alpha" prototypes of working versions.
- Evaluate: Evaluate users, target markets, competition, the design solutions, conduct field surveys, and test the initial and later designs with the target markets.
- Document: Draft white papers, user interface guidelines, specifications, and other summary documents, including marketing presentations.

The above analysis describes the essential "verbs" of the UX design profession. Over the past three decades in the HCI/UX design community, designers, analysts, educators, and theorists have identified and defined a somewhat stable, agreed-upon set of user interface components, or "nouns" on which the above verbs act, *i.e.*, the essential entities and attributes of all user interfaces, no matter what the platform of hardware and software (including operating systems and networks), user groups, contents (including vertical markets for products and services), and contexts.

User Interface Design Components

These UI components can enable developers, researchers, and critics to compare and contrast user interfaces that are evidenced on terminals, workstations, desktop computers, Websites, Web-based applications, information appliances, vehicles, mobile devices, *etc.,*. Marcus (Marcus et al. 1999; Marcus 2002b, 2009), among others, provides one way to describe these user interface components, which is strongly oriented to communication theory and to an applied theory of semiotics (Eco 1976; Pierce 1933; Innis 1985). This philosophical perspective emphasizes communication as a fundamental characteristic of computing, one that includes perceptual, formal characteristics, and dynamic, behavioral aspects about how people interact through computer-based media. Expanding upon Claude Levi-Strauss's idea of human beings as sign makers and tool makers (Levi-Strauss 2000) the theory understands a user interface as a form of dynamic, interactive visual literature as well as a suite of conceptual tools, and, as such, a cultural artifact. The user interface components are the following:

Metaphors: Metaphors are fundamental concepts communicated via words, images, sounds, and tactile experiences (Lakoff and Johnson 1980). Metaphors substitute for computer-related elements and help users understand, remember, and enjoy entities and relationships of computer-based communication systems. Metaphors can be overarching, or communicate specific aspects of user interfaces. An example of an overarching metaphor is the desktop metaphor to substitute for the computer's operating system, functions, and data. Examples of specific concepts are the trashcan, windows and their controls, pages, shopping carts, chat-rooms, and blogs (Weblogs). The pace of metaphor invention, including neologisms or verbal metaphor invention, is likely to increase because of rapid development and distribution through the Web and mobile devices of ever-changing products and services. Some researchers, such as David Gelernter, are predicting the end of the desktop metaphor era and the emergence of new fundamental metaphors (as cited, for example, in Tristram 2001).

Mental models: Mental models are structures or organizations of data, functions, tasks, roles, and people in groups at work or play. These are sometimes also called user models, cognitive models, and task models. Content, function, media, tool, role, goal, and task hierarchies are examples. They may be expressed as lists, tables, and diagrams of functions, data, and other entities, such as menus. They may be tree-structured, or more free-form.

Navigation: Navigation involves movement through the mental models, *i.e.*, through content and tools. Examples of user interface elements that facilitate such movement include those that enable dialogue, such as menus, windows, dialogue boxes, control panels, icons, and tool palettes.

Interaction: Interaction includes input/output techniques, status displays, and other feedback. Examples include the detailed behavior characteristics of keyboards, mice, pens, or microphones for input; the choices of visual display screens, loudspeakers, or headsets for output; and the use of drag and drop selection, and other action sequences.

Appearance: Appearance includes all essential perceptual attributes, *i.e.*, visual, auditory, and tactile characteristics, even olfactory in some unusual cases. Examples typically include choices of colors, fonts, animation style, verbal style (*e.g.*, verbose/terse or informal/formal), sound cues, and vibration cues.

Information Design and Information-Visualization Design

Crucial to much effective user-experience design is gathering the data, information, knowledge, and wisdom that must be interactively explored, analyzed, displayed, understood, and acted upon. Entire professional groups are devoted to information design and information visualization (plus sonification and other rarer perceptual forms of information display). Among the organizations are the Society for Technical Communication (STC), its conferences and publications and the International Institute for Information Design, with its *Information Design Journal* and associated conferences such as Vision Plus.

In these professions, similar development steps, especially user studies, task analyses, and careful design of new terminology, schema, querying, forms of reply, and other systematic approaches lead to higher level, more strategic solutions to people's needs for, desires for, and uses of information. A discussion of the field in general is contained in Marcus (2009).

Note a distinction between data and information: Computers have been called number-crunchers or data-processing machines. Nowadays, more is required, and people speak of computer-based systems for information processing, and Chief Information Officers have evolved in corporations. The following practical definitions are appropriate and useful:

- Data are significant patterns of perceptual stimuli, *e.g.*, a collection of temperature sensations or readings.
- Information is significant patterns of data, *e.g.*, the temperature and other weather conditions, or the traffic conditions for a particular road, for a particular day in a particular city.
- Knowledge is significant patterns of information together with action plans, *e.g.*, the weather conditions for a city on a particular day, their impact on traffic patterns, and the likely alternate roads on which to drive to arrive safely and on time at a destination, with a likely best choice indicated or in mind.
- Wisdom is significant patterns of knowledge, either in-born or acquired through experience, *e.g.*, the knowledge of past experience taking certain roads, the likelihood of traffic accidents or repairs along that route, and familiarity with the various route options.

Helping people make smarter decisions faster means helping them to make wise decisions, no matter what the subject domain, context, or personal experience and expertise of the user.

Of special interest are the means for communicating structures and processes, which may be shown in abstract or representational forms. Classically, these may be described as tables, forms, charts, maps, and diagrams. Many fine, classical, and thorough treatises have appeared in the past decades, such as the works of Bertin (Bertin 1967) and others.

The preceding list of graphical communication techniques suggests an approximately increasing complexity of visual syntax. This term and approach, derived from semiotics, the science of signs [see, for example, Eco (1976)], identifies four dimensions of "meaning:"

"Lexical: how are the signs produced?

Syntactic: how are the signs arranged in space and time, and with what perceptual characteristics?

Semantic: to what do the signs refer?

Pragmatic: how are the signs consumed or used?"

Combining information design and information visualization (tables, forms, charts, maps, and diagrams) in the context of designing a persuasion process means we have entered into the realm of visual and verbal rhetoric, a millennia-old system of communication that has been analyzed and practiced in the visual communication professions for centuries [see, *e.g.*, Lanham (1991)].

This book does not have space to explore all of these subjects and their ramifications for cuteness engineering or cuteness design. Readers are urged to explore further in the publications cited and recommended throughout this book. All such terms must all be reconsidered in the light of cuteness design. We consider a few specific topics below.

1.5   Market Research and Cuteness

Cuteness in all of its aspects in modern technology and in marketing can be considered among the qualities that help make products and services more successful. Marketing studies have been carried out for some campaigns that strengthen the role of cuteness for business success. Hello Kitty is perhaps one of the best known.

Among topics of marketing is branding, establishing an identity for products and services that is carried out in aspects of communication with stakeholders. Most studies of branding can be adapted to the topic of cuteness to enhance the tools of understanding which aspects of cuteness are vital for existing and new customers and which contribute to strengthen or to change the brand.

While there is no current book on marketing cuteness or cuteness branding design, we can expect these to emerge as cuteness gains traction in many countries for product/service development success.

The popularity of cuteness is shown in the numerous collections of cute imagery and cute branding collected on the Pinterest Website (www.pinterest.com). The Website currently (May 10, 2017) lists approximately 112 categories of cute images ranging across an eclectic set of expected and unexpected terms/concepts such as Carrots, Disney, Faith, Puppies, and Stuff. In each of these collections there seem to be typically 20–200 examples of cute imagery. Clearly the topic, subtopics, and imagery have grown in popularity and presumably will continue to expand in categories and examples.

One other significant measure is the growth of character design for movies, *animé*, games, and other products and services. At SIGGRAPH Asia over the past several years, and at other conferences held in Asia, there has been a noticeable increase in the number of exhibit booths of companies marketing characters and a growing number of papers and presentations about character design, many of them cute in nature. As an example of the scope and impact the Wikipedia entry (as of about May 10, 2017) for Disney/Pixar characters in feature films, shorts, and specials originally conceived by Pixar Animation Studios, a subsidiary of The Walt Disney Company since 2006, lists 286 different characters. Examples include the Abominable Snowman from "Monsters, Inc.," Francesco Bernouli from "Cars 2," Ken from "Toy Story 3," Mary from "WALL-E," and Deb from "Finding Nemo." Often major Hollywood stars add their distinctive voices to the "sound" characteristics of these cute visual creations. Each of these characters is a property that is managed (in terms of all visual, verbal, and acoustic characteristics) and designed carefully for maximum commercial success.

All of these developments suggest a growing importance for the study of the marketing and branding of cuteness.

1.6   Internationalization, Globalization, Cross-Cultural User-Experience Design, and Cuteness

As noted in Marcus and Baradit (2015), theorists of culture, anthropologists, ethnographers, and professionals in the UX field have devised descriptions of culture, proposed culture models, and explored similarities and differences of patterns of feelings, opinions, actions, signs, rituals, and values, as Hofstede and Hofstede (2005) and Schwartz (2004), among others, have described them. Marcus and Baumgartner (2004a) studied approximately 39 dimensions of culture from nine culture models that were vetted by about 60 professionals, researchers, and academics to arrive at a "Top Five" set of culture dimensions: context (high or low), technology (status of development and attitudes), uncertainty avoidance (high or low), time perception (long- *vs.* short-term, but also focusing on future, present, or past), and authority conception (high or low). Others have explored ethnographic approaches not based on culture models.

Researchers noticed differences between Chinese and Western (that is, European and North American) users: Hofstede and Hofstede (2005) use a dimension (long-term *versus* short-term time orientation) to account for a pattern of differences that seemed to occur with Confucian-influenced Asian countries versus Western countries. Van Dam and Marcus (1991) and Marcus (1993) described and visualized differences of user interface designs for North American, European, and, by implied, but unstated extension, Chinese users. Honold (1999) investigated differences between the way German and Chinese users acquire information about using mobile phones, using a mixture of Hofstede and other models, and found strong correlations between theoretical implications derived from the models and results of testing. Choong and Salvendy (1998) noted differences between US and Chinese computer science students in their mental models of the rooms of a house at home and what kinds of objects might be found in those rooms; when they gave the others' mental model to participants, they had more difficulty thinking with the mental model and made more errors. Marcus and Baumgartner (2004b) analyzed differences in business-to-business and business-to-consumer corporate Website standards for different countries (cultures) using Hofstede's dimensions as a guide; they found that there seemed to be distinctive differences in the use of imagery, thinking about size of text versus importance of the content, and other differences based on the general expectations of cultural differences. Lee (2000) considered the characteristics of a "virtual Confucian" media choices in a virtual Confucian workplace.

Dong (2007) discovered patterns of differences among Taiwanese, Korean, and US viewers of Websites, using eye-tracking equipment; the US viewers tended to scan the Website screen in a figure S or 5 shape, then relatively quickly dive into the layers of information below, while the Asian viewers tended to circle the Website page, viewing individual items more thoroughly before descending into the information architecture. Frandsen-Thorlacius et al. (2009) studied Danish *versus* Chinese users to determine that the very concept of usability differed between the two cultures. Chinese users considered "usability" more strongly possessed the attributes of "fun" and "aesthetically pleasing" than Danish users. Based, in part, on studies of participants describing what they saw in fish tanks, (Japanese viewers tended to describe relationships, US viewers tended to describe objects), Nisbett (2003) postulated major cognitive differences between the East and the West; people in these two geographic regions think differently, with Easterners seeming to possess a greater ability to consider logical opposites simultaneously without conflict. These comments are presciently described in McNeil and Freiberger's book (McNeil and Freiberger 1993) about Prof. Lofti Zadeh, who invented fuzzy set theory in the US, a theory ignored by US mathematicians and computer technology professionals, but which flourished in Japan and later Asia. According to McNeil and Freiberger, in 1993, there were about 10,000 experts of fuzzy logic in China but only a few hundred in the US.

The twenty-first century's increased exchange of products and services with China and other countries have fostered many articles and books about cross-cultural UX design. Many of these in the last 5 years are documented in an extensive bibliography compiled by Kyriakoullis and Zaphiris (2015).

As noted in Marcus and Ma (2016), theorists of culture, anthropologists, ethnographers, and professionals in the UX field have devised descriptions of culture, proposed models of culture, dimensions of culture, and explored similarities/differences of patterns of feelings, opinions, actions, signs, rituals, and values, as studied by Brejcha (2015), Dong (2007), Frandsen-Thorlacius (2009), Hofstede and Hofstede (2005), Kyriokoullis and Zaphiris (2015), Marcus (2002b), Marcus (2015b), Marcus and Baradit (2015), Marcus (2003), Marcus and Baumgartner (2004a), Nisbett (2003), Schwartz (2004), and Sun (2012). Especially important: researchers noticed differences between Eastern (Chinese, Japanese) and Western (European and North American) users in terms of learning strategies, navigation behavior, *etc.* (Frandsen-Thorlacius et al. 2009) studied Danish *versus* Chinese users to determine that the very concept of usability differed between the two cultures. Chinese users consider that "usability" more strongly possesses the attributes of "fun" and "aesthetically pleasing" built into the concept than Danish users. Based, in part, on studies of Japanese and US participants staring at fish tanks and describing what they saw (Japanese viewers tended to describe relationships, US viewers tended to describe objects), Nisbett (2003) postulated that there were major cognitive differences between the East and West; people in these two regions think differently.

The above discussion suggests that cuteness should be different in different cultures, and that cuteness in China should be of special interest.

Hints of an Emerging Chinese UX that Is Ripe for Cuteness

Publications over the past decades lead one to conclude a fundamentally Chinese UX pattern has begun to emerge, one more suitable to Chinese users than the paradigms imposed on China by Western computer technology during the past half-century. Several key moments coauthor Marcus and others' experiences point to emerging patterns:

- In 2002, Marcus saw an exhibit of the Wukong project shown at the New Paradigms in Using Computers conference, IBM Santa Theresa Laboratory, San Jose, California, USA. The Sony-Ericsson development team, together with outside consultants, which included a Chinese-American anthropologist fluent in Mandarin, designed a personal digital assistant for Chinese users that incorporated aspects of "guanxi" (关系, life-long Chinese relationship-building). Tests of the initial prototype in China showed it received superior reviews on all aspects of its design in comparison to similar offerings from US, Europe, Japan, and other sources (Marcus 2007).
- In the early 2000s, Marcus reviewed for a journal an article from Chinese sources that proposed new metaphors for Chinese software applications based on concepts derived from Chinese gardens, concepts which seemed "strange" and "foreign" Marcus surmised this may be similar to the reaction Chinese viewers originally had when first encountering Western computer technology.
- In November 2012, in Shanghai, a corporate Chinese executive speaking with Marcus conjectured that there might be a truly Chinese user-experience, which, if implemented, might make it difficult or even impossible for Western users to access and operate applications and operating systems of Chinese computer technology.
- At that same time in 2012, Marcus met Dr. Jui Shang-Ling, then Managing Director, SAP Labs China, Shanghai, who had authored two books (Jui 2007, 2010) proposing that the future of China technologically and economically lay in the prospect that China would not just manufacture (build and distribute) Chinese products and services, but would also design them.
- In (Marcus and Baradit 2015), Baradit observed over a 5-year period working in China (2009–14) the significant density and complexity of Chinese news sites and consumer portals, in which hundreds of items (images, links, buttons, text) are distributed in viewable panes, often requiring scrolling for access. In addition, the input of characters using Pinyan techniques requires intermediate options-constructs before users can proceed further to make database selections of likely characters in a string sequence. This technique seems to affect functionality of search/filters and navigation and likely has development and design implications, which should be researched further.
- Marcus observed a poster from Zhu, from China, (Zhu 2014) at the Interaction Design and Human Factors Conference 2014 (http://idhf.xrenlab.com) in Kochi, Japan, November 25–26, 2014, proposing a new metaphor for information visualization of body-sensor data that would be more effective, engaging, and

increase multi-sensory perception, based on viewing a fish in a pond, a seemingly very Chinese, or at least Asian, concept.

- In the closing keynote lecture of the User Friendly 2014 (sponsored by the User-Experience Professionals Association of China), Wuxi, China, on November 16, 2014, Prof Lou Yongxi, Dean of the College of Design and Innovation, Tongji University, presented a forceful lecture to Chinese UX designers. He urged the audience to recognize the unique circumstances of Chinese history, culture, and people, and to put that realization into action, by not just theorizing, but designing and building entirely new, inherently *Chinese* solutions to the great challenges that China now faces (Luo 2013).

The Emerging Chinese UX: Characteristics and Examples

Based on readings such as those cited above, Marcus' experience being in China on about 12 occasions since 1975, and Baradit's (Marcus and Baradit 2015) recent experience working in China for approximately 5 years, we speculate that the emerging Chinese UX will differ strongly in key characteristics. Further research may illuminate new or different characteristics for storytelling patterns, government, identity, and cuteness factors.

- **Metaphors**: As noted above, new metaphors may emerge that are fundamentally Chinese and well established in Chinese history and culture. To the Chinese, they may seem easy to understand and use, reassuring, and "natural." Chinese viewers would immediately and effortlessly understand patterns of information and knowledge, kinds of storytelling, and allusions or references. To Westerners, these same metaphors might seem foreign, unknown, unfamiliar, dysfunctional, and perhaps even threatening. Examples might include complex displays of gardens and fish ponds as stand-ins for display of large, complex systems. An example might be the status of 500 entities viewed at once, each with 7 ± 2 key characteristics, each of which might be in one, or more, or 7 ± 2 key states. The challenge would be especially great if one had to make key strategic or tactical decisions within a short time, say 30 s. Note, for example, that TenCent's new WeBank (www.webank.com) mobile banking application (with no brick-and-mortar buildings) uses simple, quick, appealing visual storytelling to explain the objects and objectives of its system, and does so with cute icons and animations. Many Chinese mobile apps use the concept of "discovery" to find new, unexpected functionality within applications.
- **Mental Models**: Mental models may emerge that are fundamental to Chinese history and culture. They may seem for Chinese users to be easy to understand and use, reassuring, and familiar, but may seem foreign, unknown, unfamiliar, and even dysfunctional to Westerners. Recall that Choong and Salvendy cited above showed users could operate more effectively and efficiently when working with familiar mental models. This observed pattern of "everything-in-one" may result from top-down or bottom-up yet-to-be-fully-analyzed social and economic forces. Grover (2014) summarizes recent Chinese mobile applications and notes they are individually accumulating more features, some of them seemingly

unrelated but appealing, while US mobile applications seem more narrow focused, minimalist, and task-driven.

A few other Chinese examples are the following: Mobile WeChat offers abundant functionality similar to WhatsApp. Besides messaging, WeChat offers video calls, a news feed, a wallet with a payments service, a Favorites feature functioning something like Evernote, a game center (with a built-in game), a location-based people finder, a "Shazam-like" song-matching service, and a mail client. Its official accounts platform provides a layer to allow hardware devices to use the app to communicate with services, instead of requiring custom apps. Baidu Maps has weather, an optional "Find My Friends" feature, travel guides, a "wallet" mode for purchasing things. Tencent Maps lets users send audio postcards. Both of them, and WeChat, have QR code readers and Groupon-style local offers. Weibo, once a Twitter analog, does much more. Its "Post" button allows one to post up to 10 distinct types of content, from blog entry to restaurant review. Weibo, also, has a wallet feature.

- **Navigation**: Navigation schema, as noted above, may emerge that are fundamental to Chinese history and, for Chinese users, may be easy to understand and use, reassuring, and familiar, but may seem foreign, unknown, unfamiliar, and dysfunctional to Westerners. The ability and/or preference for large displays of information that encourages a "tour of the surface," so evident in traditional Chinese painting, calligraphy, and typography, may suggest such a distinction that is supported in Dong's eye-tracking experiments cited above.

- **Interaction**: New interaction paradigms may emerge that are fundamental to Chinese history and culture. These preferences may seem foreign, unknown, unfamiliar, and dysfunctional to Westerners, but they would be easy to understand and use, reassuring, and familiar, enabling Chinese users to work with character displays, visual attributes, sound, and other input/output techniques more effectively. In a recent summary of Chinese mobile applications by Grover (2014) he comments that voice messaging in chat applications such as WeChat is popular because it removes the challenge of typing, can be used by older users without much computer proficiency, and may assist large numbers of people with limited literacy.

- **Appearance**: New visual appearance characteristics may appear that are fundamental to Chinese history and culture. Consider the traditional decorations of architecture, vases, paintings, and calligraphy that are quite different from either baroque/rococo European painting or the minimalist traditions of the Bauhaus and Swiss-German Typography of the twentieth century. In addition, the frequency of cute mascots, icons, animations, and storytelling seem to indicate a unique Asian, sometimes specifically Chinese approach. Example of Chinese cuteness can be found throughout cities, publications, Websites, and applications.

There are a few additional key differentiators to consider:

- **Space**: In his closing keynote lecture of the User Friendly 2014 conference in Wuxi, China, Prof. Lou Yongxi, cited above, spoke of the great spaces of China as a key context and challenge. The scale of some public visual displays seems at times quite extraordinary. China as a land mass is only 90,000 square miles smaller (about the size of the US state of Michigan), and cultural history has shown the influence of the "wide open spaces" in the US on its technology, society, and culture. Chinese UX solutions may emerge that emphasize large, public displays or the traversal of large virtual spaces as giant two-dimensional experiences before "descending" into layers below, in other words, flatter hierarchies. This approach was tried in the 1960s in the US when the Architecture Machine Group at MIT, under the leadership of Nicholas Negroponte, with Richard Bolt, designed and implemented its Spatial Database Management System (Brand 1987). The approach featured a large virtual space that one could review on a wall-sized display viewed from the comfort of an "executive" reclining chair. However, this approach never caught on like the Xerox PARC, Apple, Microsoft versions of graphical user interfaces. The difference in the Chinese approach to depicting large, dense visual spaces of text, imagery, and controls is already evident in Web shopping sites associated with Singles Day, November 1, 2014, the largest single transaction day in world history (US$8.18b, RMB50b). Subsequent Singles Days have demonstrated continuing growth in the amount of money transacted.
- **Time**: Few countries/cultures can claim the 4000 years of Chinese heritage, which is in a position today to be a major player in world markets, technology, society, politics, and culture. This perspective gives China a unique "view" of the word and its time scale. This may present itself in time scales of information displays, the time that it takes for information to travel throughout its society, *etc.* In addition, due to specific governmental and social contexts, in China some activities may go more slowly in order to be considered "valid" or "official." Quicker is not always better. As the Wukong project pointed out (Marcus 2007), US business relations focus on doing business quickly and maybe becoming friends later, while the Chinese approach emphasizes taking one's time to become friends and then maybe doing business.
- **Scale**: On the occasion of visiting the central China city of Xian for the first time, Marcus asked a tour guide how many people lived in Xian. The guide replied, "Oh, it is a small city, about 7 million people." This difference of "small cities" in the US *versus* China seems significant. With more than four times the population of the US, solutions to large scale seem imperative. This may lead to unique solutions for how to handle large amounts of participants and money in Internet purchase/pay systems, how to deal with social media networks significantly larger than any existing today (with all the differences of privacy, personality, and context).

All of the above factors can inter-relate to cuteness. The dynamic growth of China and the spread of Chinese products/services, including the growing influence on media, such as movies, imply that cuteness in China should be studied more carefully in relation to all of user-experience dimensions.

1.7 Personas and Cuteness

User-centered design focuses attention on the users, especially the user types. These are often termed personas or user profiles. A persona is not an actual user, but a "pretend user" or a "hypothetical archetype" (Cooper 2004). Personas can assist in keeping specific users vividly in the minds of developers throughout the development process. They are "fictional" collections of key characteristics of key users but based on known facts or trends. Typically, UI development teams define one to nine primary personas.

A persona is defined by stating a set of objectives/goals distinct from other personas, such that their measures of a successful user interface and task flow will vary according to their needs and interests. Although there are many *persons* who may use the product, the best designs tend to be focused rather than diluted. This focus can be achieved only by optimizing the design toward a few key personas. Personas are also helpful in optimizing sections of the software towards the user types that will use the product.

Personas typically state/show the following:

- Name, age, title, slogan of the Persona
- Image of the Persona (photograph, sketch, cartoon, *etc.*)
- Context (physical, social, cognitive, emotional, cultural, *etc.*)
- Objectives/goals (personal, professional, communal)
- Impacts on the design.

In describing personas, their connection to cuteness should be mentioned. Some personas may be very positive, others neutral, and some very negative. The persona's characteristics would affect strategies for making products and services more appealing.

As noted above, personas typically list key characteristics, behaviors, context (physical, emotional, cognitive, social, *etc.*), and the impact on design. Cuteness could, in theory, be attached to any or all of these attributes.

1.8 Use Scenarios and Cuteness

Use scenarios are a UX/UI development technique whereby, during the development of a prototype to simulate the major characteristics of a software product, UX designers write a use scenario to determine what behavior will be simulated.

A scenario is essentially a sequence of task flows with actual content provided, such as the user's demographics and goals, the details of the information being worked with, *etc*. Note that use scenarios differ from *use cases*, which is a term used in the world of software development. Use cases are detailed descriptions of tasks that list or describe specific functions of a software application and the data input/out related to these functions. The use case is often somewhat technical in nature and a step further away from software code itself than so-called pseudocode. Use scenarios, on the other hand, are usually descriptions in everyday language, not in deeply technical terminology.

For example, to simulate a Print dialogue box, a scenario might state that "an account executive wants to print out a Powerpoint presentation in landscape format, duplexed, with page numbers, as quickly as possible." The prototype developer then needs to simulate, with prototyping software, how the account executive would accomplish this task using the software.

Scenarios typically should have a format that includes the following:

- A descriptive and compelling title
- The background of the situation and the user
- The event or information that prompts user action
- Step-by-step listing of user actions (typically technology-independent) to reach a goal or conclusion
- A list of user benefits demonstrated by the scenario
- Optionally, reference to any supporting materials such as existing screen designs, paper materials, information listings, or prototypes
- Optionally, a description of the current methods used to accomplish the same goal. These descriptions are good for comparison, because the new scenario is meant to be an improvement upon the existing methods.

As noted, user scenarios describe typical, high-profile functions and data within products/services. Use scenarios involving cuteness would need to describe specific activities that incorporate cuteness. More importantly, it would be appropriate to indicate how cuteness helps the user accomplish tasks or to be more engaged with the product/service because of the existence of cute characteristics.

For example, in the world of mobile apps, cuteness might cause users to notice mobile app displays more because the cute characters or scenes or interactions would attract their attention more directly and more strongly. Subsequently, cute characters, icons, or other figures might make functions/icons more memorable, or even clarify them. Cute interactions, such as verbal cues to the device, cute comments from the device, might keep users engaged and functioning in a productive manner.

Consider, for example, a familiar, cute character that might represent a training or motivational character that would urge users to continue their progress in climbing through a virtual reality terrain that is challenging and (virtually) potentially dangerous, *e.g.,* climbing along a precarious face of a rock wall, with a drop of thousands of virtual feet below. Cute characters could be helpful, reassuring, charming, and calming.

In China, the application called WeBank uses a brief set of cute screen designs to explain how its product works. This approach is a typically Chinese one: lots of graphical imagery, minimal text, and focus on dynamic cute animated screen designs.

1.9   Persuasion Theory and Cuteness

Some products/services attempt to use persuasion theory to change people's behavior. A series of such design are described in Marcus' book *Mobile Persuasion Design* (Marcus 2015a, b). In describing the theory, or science of persuasion, Cialdini's work (Cialdini 2001, 2007) should be considered. Cialdini concentrates particularly on the psychological dimensions concerned in the act of persuasion: What makes an individual comply with another's request? What makes someone change or adapt new attitudes or actions? Cialdini distinguishes six basic phenomena in human behavior, which are supposed to favor positive reactions to persuasive messages of others: reciprocation, consistency, social validation, liking, authority and scarcity. These tendencies in the social influence process are characteristic of human nature and are thus valid across national boundaries; nevertheless, cultural norms, traditions, and experiences can have an impact on the relative weight of each of the six mentioned factors, which Cialdini points out.

In addition, Fogg has made significant contributions to persuasion-related research (Fogg 2003; Fogg and Eckles 2007).

In alignment with Fogg's persuasion theory, Marcus defined five key processes to achieve behavioral change via a Machine's functions and data:

- Attract users via traditional marketing techniques, that is, making users aware and motivating them to examine the application
- Increase frequency of using the application
- Motivate users to change some habits, for example, interaction with and openness towards the subject matter and people, experience and observation of differences in experience, and ways of documenting changes
- Teach users how to change habits
- Persuade users to change habits (short-term change)
- Persuade users to change general approach to objectives, people, objects, contexts, obstacles, emotions (long-term, or life-style change).

Each step has requirements for an application.

Motivation is a need, want, interest, or desire that propels someone in a certain direction. From the sociobiological perspective, people in general tend to maximize reproductive success and ensure the future of descendants. We apply this theory in the Machine by making people understand that a determinate behavior can fundamentally enrich their daily experiences, that it can increase their knowledge and understanding, and that it can ultimately trigger a process of relationship building to improve success.

One may also draw on Maslow's Theory of Human Motivation (Maslow 1943), which he based on his analysis of fundamental human needs. We adapted these needs to each Machine context.

Safety and security: met by the assistance through family, friends, or advisors; and by the provision of obstacles-, fun-, human-contact-, and others-related information, tips, and advice.

Belonging and love: expressed through social sharing and support among friends and family.

Esteem: satisfied by social comparisons that display progress and destination expertise, as well as by self-challenges that are suggested by the application and that display the goal-accomplishment processes.

Self-actualization: fulfilled by being able to follow and retrace continuous progress and advancement in a personal diary.

Many publications on persuasion and technology have appeared in recent years. One such compendium is the *Proceedings of Persuasive Technology* 2015 (MacTavish and Basapour 2015), the tenth anniversary conference on the subject.

It seems likely that cuteness can make persuasive arguments, persuasive functions, persuasive data, and motivational messages more effective. Like humor, cuteness may help learning and developing a positive attitude toward new behaviors, thoughts, and feelings.

1.10 Metaphor Design and Cuteness

As noted earlier, metaphors, using one thing to stand for another, is a familiar rhetorical technique and a familiar component of computer-based products and services. It seems likely that many familiar metaphorical constructs in computer-based products and services, as well as other contexts, can have cute versions. For example, the desktop metaphor of most computer systems can be presented in a cute, illustrative, even childlike fashion, as is sometimes used for children's computers. Many years ago, a researcher reporting in SIGGRAPH proceedings demonstrated an application that could automatically construct comic-book-like imagery of conversations taking place in interactive communications.

For both existing, older metaphors, new metaphors currently evolving, and future metaphors that are yet to be invented, cute variations seem quite feasible and potentially helping to spread the knowledge of and adoption of new metaphorical constructs. It seems possible that cute metaphors might assist applications and content "going viral" because of the potential appeal of cute imagery.

1.11 Information Architecture Design (Mental Model and Navigation) and Cuteness

As noted earlier, mental models (the structure of all content) and navigation (ways of moving through the mental models) are fundamental components of all user interfaces and user-experiences. It seems challenging to imagine what cute information architecture might be. However, one can imagine organizations or structures that feature cute elements or components, cute names, and cute images representing key features. As with cute metaphors, cute mental models and cute navigation may assist in bringing about the more rapid assimilation of new products and services.

1.12 Look-and-Feel Design (Appearance and Interaction) and Cuteness

Cute appearance and interaction characteristics seem easy to imagine, and many have been employed already in children's software and products, as well as in personal robots and even commercial robots.

Cute robots have been pioneered in Japan, also designed in the USA and China, and deployed throughout the world. Now robots are increasingly being used in China, where "machine people" are rolling into restaurants and banks, but can't be trusted with heavy dishes yet (Chen 2016). Articles have appeared that show elderly people in Japan are soothed and comforted by cute robot animals. It seems likely that such use of cuteness will expand considerably in the years ahead, especially for countries like Japan with large numbers of seniors. A *Wall Street Journal* article reported about a cute robot makes screeching sound to drive away children because it must get back to work being a security guard in a shopping mall in the US (Wells 2016).

Even cute sounds can have a role in the design of products and services. They can accompany icons, or movements of objects, or accompany specific user actions or computer feedback. Many decades ago, Bill Gaver pioneered the concept of earcons (Gaver 1989) the use of sound to indicate activities in HCI and the characteristics of specific depicted objects. For example, moving an object across the desktop made a characteristic scraping sound. If a large file were dropped into the Trashcan, it made a louder noise of a certain kind that a small file. At that time, no reference to cuteness was mentioned or perhaps even imagined, but Disney cartoons have used cute sounds to accompany crashes, people bumping into each other, and moving quickly (running people, racing autos, *etc.*).

Already the Apple iPhone 6 offers alternative voices for Siri, including British, Australian, and US accents. Charming cartoon characters like Yoda and Homer Simpson may follow. In the Waze GPS Navigation app on the iPhone, it is possible to substitute the Hollywood star Morgan Freeman's voice. For example, information about the Star Wars voice app appears at http://gadgets.ndtv.com/apps/features/ from-yoda-speak-to-darth-vader-voice-changer-the-force-is-strong-with-these-apps-779230, and information about the Morgan Freeman voice substitution appears at http://www.idigitaltimes.com/how-get-morgan-freeman-voice-waze-gps-navigation-app-google-makes-maps-directions-514180. It seems likely that it is only a matter of time that users will be able to enjoy Siri speaking in the voice of Bugs Bunny, Daffy Duck, Tweety Bird, or even Elmer Fudd, as examples of the inevitable "cutification" of Siri's voice.

Recent articles have appeared about viv.com, an AI company purchased by Samsung, which makes an eponymous software that uses voice for all communication (Cheng and Jeong 2016).

In Marcus' personal discussions in 2016 with Adam Cheyer, one of Viv's cofounders, Cheyer suggested that most interactions in future HCI would be through voice, and that their AI software would be an excellent and complete platform for all such interactions. This technology opens up a large opportunity for cute sounds, cute voices, and other forms of cute sonification of data, functions, and interactions.

The viral success of Pokémon Go was based in part on its collection of cute monsters hiding virtually in public places, which users could seek out, capture, and use in the game (see www.pokemon.com and https://en.wikipedia.org/wiki/Pokémon_Pikachu for examples.

Many technology companies employ cute animals as mascots, especially, but not only, in east Asia. For example, Lang (2014) documented two dozen tech mascots with unusual eyes, spikes, or wings. The familiar cute Android robot from Google and the Baidu Bear are typical examples.

1.13 Cuteness Guidelines

Many companies that produce cute products, services, publications, and brands, such as Disney and Sanrio, do not regularly publish detailed information about the cuteness-design guidelines that make their designs so effective. One known major high-technology company that has published design guidelines is Baidu (Wang et al. 2014).

Another, limited source of cuteness guidelines is Preuss' "The Elements of Cute Character Design" (Preuss 2010). Space does not permit extensive listing of the recommendations, but topics include the following:

Definition of cuteness: childlike, sweet, helplessness
Childlike characteristics: large round heads; large eyes; small or absent mouths

Arms and legs: short, round, soft, unmuscular
Roundness: used throughout
Simple: avoid complexity
Little and lovable: small-sized, sociable
Colors: warm, friendly, soft contrasts.

For all such guidelines, it remains to be determined how culturally biased such prescriptions must be. Metrics are yet to be determined; much research remains.

1.14   Examples of Cuteness in UX of Computer-Based Products/Services

The following examples (Fig. 1.5) show cuteness incorporated into computer-based products and services, including appearance and functions.

Fig. 1.5 Cute guidelines pages from the Baidu UX design guidelines (Wang et al. 2014) featuring specific comments about cuteness (used with permission from Baidu)

1.15   Concluding Comments

This chapter is intended to introduce many of the terms and themes of cuteness engineering and cuteness design. Although cuteness engineering has emerged in many forms of product/service design, we have focused on computer-based products and services and in some cases specifically the user interface and/or the user-experience. We focus on this aspect because it has taken some years to emerge as an important subtopic of user-experience design and because its growth in the coming years seems important. Some of the terms, themes, and historical references will be discussed in greater detail in later chapters.

In this chapter, we have introduced a conceptual framework for the user-centered design process. In any future development team's attempting to "cutify" a product or service, these concepts, steps, and methods would have to be employed to ensure better success of that development.

We have also focused on China regarding this subject because the country and the culture seem poised to produce and consume more cuteness than perhaps any nation on earth. According to the August 27, 2016 version of *Business Insider* (www.businessinsider.com/chinas-middle-class-is-exploding-2016-8), the urban population of China is 730 million people, and the site refers to a study consulting firm McKinsey & Company that China's middle class will consist of 76 percent of China's urban population by 2022, where middle class is defined as urban households that earn US$9,000–US$34,000 a year. Already Hollywood movies and many major Silicon Valley product developers like Apple keep a sharp eye on the needs and wants of the Chinese market. It seems likely that cuteness engineering likewise will be strongly influenced by the "China factor" in the near and medium term.

Although we planned to have a chapter on cuteness design guidelines, we have not included such a chapter. There are a few documents guiding the design of cute characters or figures or objects such as that of Preuss (Preuss 2010) and the brief guidelines of the Baidu UX document (Wang et al. 2014). As later chapters on the history and significance of cuteness in Japan and China will show, cuteness has a different and complex history that differs from that of the West. It seems likely that future guidelines for cuteness will have to acknowledge the particular time, culture, context of use, and media to be most effective. Already styleguides mentioned in the interview of Hello Kitty's designer in Chap. 5 point in this direction.

When coauthor Marcus first published an article about cuteness in the user interface/user-experience world (Marcus 2002c), there were relatively few publications focusing on this topic. Since that time, there have been many more, including Portigal (2003), Cheok et al. (2007), Bao et al. (2015), Wang et al. (2015), No Author (2015), and Laohakangvalvit et al. (2016). In May of 2017, the ACM Digital Library returned 109 documents for a search on "cuteness." More research, evaluation, and design seem certain to appear.

In the world of cuteness engineering, including cuteness design, analysis, evaluation, research, and planning, we have much to learn about what cuteness is, was, and will be. We hope you enjoy and learn from the following chapters.

Acknowledgements The preceding chapter contains extensive abridged and merged text from three publications by one author, Marcus (together with the co-author Ma for one source), all published by Springer and used with permission of the publisher and the authors [Marcus (2015a, b), Marcus and Baradit (2015), Marcus and Xiaojuan (2016)].

References

Alley T (1981) Head shape and the perception of cuteness. Dev Psychol 17(5):650–654. doi:10. 1037/0012-1649.17.5.650

(Anonymous). Cuteness. https://en.wikipedia.org/wiki/Cuteness, viewed on 06 Dec 2016

Bao Y, Yang J, Cao L, Li H, Tang J (2015) Cuteness recognition and localization in the photos of animals. In: Proceedings of 22nd ACM international conference on Multimedia, Orlando, Florida, 03–07 Nov 2014, pp 1193–1196. ISBN: 978-1-4503-3063-3. doi:10.1145/2647868. 2655046

Bertin J (1983) Semiology of graphics: diagrams, networks, maps. Madison, WI. Originally published in French as *Semiologie graphique*, Edition Guathier-Villars, Paris, and republished in 2011 by Esri Press, Redlands, California

Boyle J, Kao W-C (eds) (2016) The Retro-Futurism of cuteness. Punctum Books, punctum-books.com, Online book at http://retrofuturismofcuteness.net. Reviews at http://premoderncuteness.academic.wlu.edu (checked 08 Dec 2016)

Brand S (1987) Nicholas Negroponte and Richard Bolt, the Spatial Data Management System (SDMS), as described in *The Media Lab*: *Inventing the Future at M.I.T.* New York: Viking-Penguin, especially, p 138

Brejcha J (2015) Cross-cultural human-computer interaction and user-experience design: a semiotic perspective. CRC Press, Boca Raton, Florida

Chen, Te-Ping (2016) In China, a robot's place is in the kitchen. Wall Str J A1ff, 25 Jul 2016

Cheng J, Jeong E-Y (2016) Samsung buys artificial-intelligence startup founded by Siri creators: Samsung electronics said …it will buy Viv Labs, founded by the creators of Apple's Siri service. Online source http://www.wired.com/2014/08/viv/. Updated Oct 6, 2016 6:54 am ET

Cheok AD, Inami M, Fernando ONN, Inakage M, Merritt TR (2007) Explorations on interactive interfaces using cuteness. In: Proceedings of 2nd international conference on digital interactive media in entertainment and arts, Perth, Australia, 19–21 Sep 2007, pp 3–3. ISBN: 978-1-59593-708-7. doi:10.1145/1306813.1306818

Choong Y, Salvendy G (1998) Designs of icons for use by Chinese in mainland China, In Interacting with computers. Int J Hum Comp Interact 9(4):417–430. Elsevier, Amsterdam Feb 1998,

Cialdini RB (2001) The science of persuasion. Sci Am 284:76–81. (www.influenceatwork.com) 2 Feb 2001

Cialdini RB (2007) Influence: the psychology of persuasion. Revised Edition. Harper, New York

Cooper A (2004) The inmates are running the asylum. SAMS, Indianapolis. ISBN 0-672-31649-8

Dong Y (2007) A cross-cultural comparative study on users' perception of the webpage: with the focus on cognitive style of Chinese, Korean, and American. Master's Thesis, Department of Industrial Design, Korea Advanced Institute of Science and Technology. Seoul, Korea. 113 pp Uses eye-tracking to discern patterns of Web-page viewing

Eco U (1976) A theory of semiotics. Indiana University Press, Bloomington

Fogg BJ (2003) Persuasive technology: using computers to change what we think and do. Morgan Kaufmann Publishers, San Francisco

Fogg BJ, Eckles D (2007). Mobile persuasion: 20 perspectives of the future of behavior change. Persuasive Technology Lab, Stanford University, Palo Alto, CA

Frandsen-Thorlacius O, Hornbæk K, Hertzum M, Clemmensen T (2009) Non-universal usability? A survey of how usability is understood by Chinese and Danish users. Proc. Conf Hum Factors Comp Sys 2009:41–58

Gaver WM (1989) The sonicfinder: an interface that uses auditory icons. J Hum Comp Interact 4:1 67–94, Mar 1989

Grover D (2014) Chinese mobile app UI trends. http://dangrover.com/blog/2014/12/01/chinese-mobile-app-ui-trends.html. Checked 05 Jan 2015

Hartson R, Pyla P (2012) The UX book: process and guidelines for ensuring a quality user experience. Morgan Kaufmann (Elsevier), Waltham, MA

Hofstede G, Hofstede GJ (2005) Cultures and organizations: software and the mind. McGraw-Hill, New York

Honold P (1999). Learning how to use a cellular phone: comparison between German and Chinese users. J Soc Tech Commun 46(2):196–205, May 1999

Innis, RE (1985) Semiotics: an introductory anthology. Indiana University Press

Jui S-L (2007) *From Made in China to Invented in China* (in Chinese). Beijing: Publishing House of Electronics Industry, p 192

Jui S-L (2010) Innovation in China: the Chinese software industry. London and New York: Routledge/Taylor and Francis Group, p 170

Karraker K, Stern M (1990) Infant physical attractiveness and facial expression: effects on adult perceptions. Basic Appl Soc Psychol 11(4):371–385. doi:10.1207/s15324834basp1104_2

Koyama R, Takahashi Y, Mori K (2006) Assessing the cuteness of children: significant factors and gender differences. Soc Behav Personal 34(9):1087–1100. doi:10.2224/sbp.2006.34.9.1087

Kyriakoullis L, Zaphiris P (2015) Culture and HCI: a review of recent cultural studies in HCI and social networks. Univ Access Inf Soc 15(4):629–642, Nov 2016

Lakoff G, Johnson M (1980) Metaphors we live by. The University of Chicago Press, Chicago

Lanham RA (1991) A handlist of rhetorical terms, 2nd edn. University of California Press, Berkeley. ISBN 0-520-07668-0

Lang A (2014). 24 tech mascots with eyes, spikes or wings. Rewind and capture, 20 Aug 2014. http://www.rewindandcapture.com/24-tech-mascots-with-eyes-spikes-or-wings/. Checked 5 Jan 2016)

Laohakangvalvit T, Achalakul T, Ohkura M (2016) Kawaii feeling estimation by product attributes and biological signals. In: Proceedings ACM International Conference on Multimodal Interaction, Tokyo, Japan, 12–16 Nov 2016, pp 563–56. ISBN: 978-1-4503-4556-9. doi:10.1145/2993148.2997621

Lee O (2000) The role of cultural protocol in media choice in a confucian virtual workplace. IEEE Trans Prof Commun 43(2):196–200

Levi-Strauss C (2000) Structural anthropology. Basic Books, Trans. Claire Jacobson and Brooke Schoepf. New York

Luo Y, Valsecchi F, Diaz C (2013) Design Harvests: An Acupunctural Design Approach Towards Sustainability. Shanghai: Studio Tao, p 321

MacTavish T, Basapur S (eds) (2015) Persuasive Technology. In: Proceedings of the 10th International Conference, Chicago, IL, USA, 3–5 June 2015. London: Springer

Maslow AH (1943) A theory of human motivation. Psychol Rev 50:370–396

Marcus A (1993) Human communication issues in advanced UIs. Commun ACM 36(4):101–109

Marcus A (2002a) Information visualization for advanced vehicle displays. Inf Vis 1:95–102

Marcus A (2002b) Globalization, localization, and cross-cultural communication in user-interface design. In Jacko J, Spears A (eds) Chapter 23 Handbook of Human-computer interaction. Lawrence Erlbaum Publishers, New York, pp 441–463

Marcus A (2002c) The cult of cute: the challenge of user-experience design. Interact 9(6):29–34. doi:10.1145/581951.581966

Marcus A (2003) User-Interface Design and China: A Great Leap Forward. Fast-Forward Column.
    Interact, ACM Publisher, http://www.acm.org, 10(1), January/February 2003, pp. 21–25
Marcus A (2007) Wukong Project, mentioned in Marcus' Tutorial Description "cross-cultural
    user-experience design," user friendly 2007 conference, Beijing, China. http://www.upachina.
    org/userfriendly2007/pwcontent/w_Aaron_en.html. Last Checked 28 Dec 2014
Marcus A (2009) Integrated information systems. Inf Des J 17(1):4–21
Marcus A (2015a). Mobile persuasion design: changing behaviour by combining persuasion
    design with information design. Springer UK, London. ISBN 978-1-4471-6744-0, © 2015,
    658 pp. SpringerLink http://link.springer.com/book/10.1007%2F978-1-4471-6744-0
Marcus A (2015b) HCI and user-experience design. Springer, London
Marcus A, Baradit S (2015). Emerging Chinese user-experience design. In: Proceedings design,
    user experience, and usability conference, 02–07 Aug 2015, Los Angeles, CA, USA. In HCII
    2015 Proceedings in Springer, London. http://2015.hci.international/proceedings
Marcus A, Baumgartner V (2004a) A practical set of culture dimension for evaluating
    user-interface   designs.   In   Proceedings   of   Sixth   Asia-Pacific   Conference   on
    Computer-Human Interaction (APCHI 2004), Royal Lakeside Novotel Hotel, Rotorua, New
    Zealand, 30 Jun–2 July 2004, pp 252–261
Marcus A, Baumgartner V. (2004b). Mapping User-Interface design components vs. culture
    dimensions in corporate websites. Vis Lang J. MIT Press, pp 1–65
Marcus A, Ma X (2016). Cuteness design: an initial analysis. In: Proceedings of design, user
    experience, and usability conference, Toronto, 17–22 Jul 2016. In HCII 2016 Proceedings.
    Springer, London. http://2016.hci.international/proceedings
Marcus A, et al (1999) Globalization of user-interface design for the web. In: Proceedings of
    human factors and the web conference, Gaithersburg, MD, 3 Jun 1999. http://zing.ncsl.nist.
    gov/hfweb/proceedings/marcus/. Checked on 16 Sept 2014
McNeill D, Freiberger P (1993) Fuzzy logic: the revolutionary computer technology that is
    changing our world. Simon and Schuster, New York
Nisbett RE (2003) The geography of thought: how Asians and westerners think differently…and
    why. Free Press, New York
No   Author   (2015)   DreamWorks   animation   presents   'HOME':   just   another
    post-apocalyptic-alien-invasion-buddy-road movie?" In: Proceedings of ACM SIGGRAPH
    2015 computer animation festival, Los Angeles, California, 09–13 Aug 1015, pp 172–172.
    ISBN: 978-1-4503-3326-9. doi:10.1145/2773215.2773229
Peirce CS (1933) Existential Graphs, pp 293–470. In: Hartshome, Weiss (eds) The Collected
    Papers of Charles Sanders Peirce. See Peirce, Charles Sanders. Collected papers. Vols 1–6
    edited by Charles Hartshorne and Paul Weiss; vols 7–8 edited by A.W. Burks. Belknap Press
    of Harvard University Press, Cambridge, 1958–1966. http://www.nlx.com/collections/95.
    Checked 11 Sept 2014. See also, http://plato.stanford.edu/entries/peirce-semiotics/. Checked
    11 Sept 2014
Portigal S (2003). Kawaii: adventures in a parallel universe. Proceedings of Designing for User
    Experiences (DUX) 2003 Conference, San Francisco, CA, 06–07 Jun 2003, ACM, NY. pp 1–
    4. ISBN:1-58113-728-1. doi:10.1145/997078.997110
Preuss S (2010) The elements of cute character design. 12 Apr 2010. http://design.tutsplus.com/
    articles/the-elements-of-cute-character-design–vector-3533. Checked 5 Jan 2016
Schneider A (10 Jan 2013). Agreed, baby pandas are cute. But Why? National public radio.
    Retrieved 13 Jan 2013, also: article dated 20 Jan 2013, http://www.npr.org/sections/thetwo-
    way/2013/01/10/169057467/agreed-baby-pandas-are-cute-but-why. Checked 09 Dec 16
Schwartz SH (2004) Mapping and interpreting cultural differences around the world. In: Vinken H,
    Soeters J, Ester P (eds) Comparing cultures, dimensions of culture in a comparative
    perspective. Brill, Leiden, The Netherlands, pp 43–73
Sprengelmeyer R, Perrett D, Fagan E, Cornwell R, Lobmaier J, Sprengelmeyer A, Aasheim H,
    Black I, Cameron L, Crow S, Milne N, Rhodes E, Young A (2009) The cutest little baby face:
    a hormonal link to sensitivity to cuteness in infant faces. Psychol Sci 20(9):149–154

Suddath C (2008) A brief history of mickey mouse *Time*, 18 Nov 2008. http://content.time.com/time/arts/article/0,8599,1859935,00.html. Checked 08 Nov 2015

Sun H (2012). Cross-cultural technology design. Oxford, New York

Tristram C (2001) The next computer interface. Technology Review, Dec 2001, pp 53–59

Van Dam A, Marcus A (1991) User-interface developments for the nineties. Computer 24(9): 49–57

Van Duuren M, Kendell-Scott L, Stark N (2003) Early aesthetic choices: infant preferences for attractive premature infant faces. Int J Behav Dev 27(3):212–219. doi:10.1080/01650250244000218

Waldman K (2015). The totally adorable history of cute. Slate. 27 Feb 2015. http://www.slate.com/blogs/lexicon_valley/2015/02/27/cute_etymology_and_history_from_sharp_keen_or_shrewd_to_charming_and_attractive.html. Viewed 09 Dec 2016

Wang W et al. Baidu UX Department (2014) Baidu UX Design Guidelines (in Chinese). Baidu, Beijing, p 234

Wang K, Nguyen Tam V, Feng J, Sepulveda J (2015) Sense beyond expressions: cuteness. In: Proceedings of 23rd ACM international conference on Multimedia, Brisbane, Australia, 226–30 Oct 2015, pp 1067-1070. ISBN: 978-1-4503-3459-4. doi:10.1145/2733373.2806283

Wells G (2016). Too cute for their own good, robots get self-defense instincts. Wall Street J, A1ff, 21 Jun 2016

Zhu B (Tina) (2014) Designing bio-data displays for appreciating the body." Poster, in *Proceedings* of on memory stick distributed to participants, interaction design and human factors conference 2014, Kochi, Japan, 25–26 Nov 2014

Chapter 2
Cuteness in Japan

2.1 Cuteness and *Kawaii*

2.1.1 "Kawaii" as a Translation of "Cute"

In this chapter, the Japanese word "*kawaii*" will be discussed instead of "cute" because the Japanese do not use the English word "cuteness" or "cute" in their conversation or in written form and "*kawaii*" is the closest word to "cute." English–Japanese dictionary (Takebayashi and Azuma 2003) defines the word "cute" as (1) *kawaii* (cute, pretty), *kireina* (beautiful), (2) *Rikouna* (intelligent), *nukemeno-nai* (shrewd, smart), *hashikoi* (shrewd, clever), *kiga-kiku* (clever). This definition corresponds to entries in typical English dictionaries now available in the U.S. and the U.K.

2.1.2 The Word "Cute"

According to *The American Heritage Dictionary of the English Dictionary (5th ed.)* (Nichols et al. 2011), "Cute was originally a shortened form of acute in the sense 'keenly perceptive or discerning, shrewd.' In this sense, cute is first recorded in a dictionary published in 1731. Probably cute came to be used as a term of approbation for things demonstrating acuteness or ingenious design, and so it went on to develop its own sense of 'pretty feeling'".

In *A Dictionary of the English Language* (Johnson 1755) by Samuel Johnson, there is no "cute" but just acute with the meaning "(1) Sharp, ending in a point, opposed to obtuse or blunt, (2) In a figurative sense applied to men, ingenious, penetrating, opposed to dull or stupid, (3) Spoken of the senses, vigorous, powerful in operation, (4) Acute disease, (5) Acute accent."

In summary, the English word "cute" means something that draws people's attention sharply in an attractive and emotional way.

© Springer International Publishing AG 2017
A. Marcus et al., *Cuteness Engineering*, Springer Series on Cultural Computing,
DOI 10.1007/978-3-319-61961-3_2

2.1.3 "Kawaii" Without the Meaning of Acuteness

In contrast, the Japanese word "*kawaii*" does *not* have the meaning of acuteness at all. Compared to the notion of acuteness, "*kawaii*" means simply to be attractive and soft. It is not related to intelligence at all. Instead, the word is more similar to the term "pretty."

In English dictionaries, "cute" and "pretty" are defined as follows:

Cute

– Attractive or pretty in a youthful or dainty way (American Heritage 5th ed. 2011).
– Having a pleasing and usually youthful appearance (Merriam Webster's 2017).
– Pleasingly pretty or dainty (Random House 1967).
– Delightfully pretty or dainty (American Heritage Student's Dictionary 1986).
– Acute, clever, sharp, shrewd (1731), U.S. cunning (1868) (Shorter OED 1959).
– Charmingly pretty, sweet. (N.AM.) clever, shrewd (Paperback OED 7th ed. 2012).
– Attractive. Smart in a way that can seem rude (Longman 2004).
– (none) (Johnson 1755).

Pretty

– Pleasing or attractive in a graceful or delicate way (American Heritage 5th ed. 2011).
– Attractive to look at usually in a simple or delicate way (Merriam Webster's 2017).
– Pleasing or attractive to the eye in a feminine or childlike way (Random House 1967).
– Pleasing or appealing in a delicate way (AH Student's Dictionary 1986).
– Beautiful in a slight, dainty, or diminutive way of women or children (1440) (Shorter OED 1959).
– Having an attractive or pleasant appearance (Paperback OED 7th ed. 2012)
– A woman or child who is pretty is attractive. Attractive or pleasant to look at or listen to (Longman 2004).
– Neat, elegant, pleasing without surprise or elevation (Johnson 1755).

As shown above, even in English, the meaning of acute (sharp, shrewd, and clever) seems almost to have been lost today, and cute is similar to pretty. If this is true, *kawaii* can also be used as the translation of cute as well as pretty.

kawaii is now included in OED (Oxford...2010) as follows:

(a) Adjective. Cute, esp. in a manner considered characteristic of Japanese popular culture; charming, darling; ostentatiously adorable.
(b) Noun. That which is *kawaii*; cuteness.

But to co-author Kurosu, primary author of this chapter, who is a Japanese, it is not clear how English-speaking people today differentiate the use of "cute" and "pretty," and it is still unclear which of the terms "cute" and "pretty" will match better to the meaning of "*kawaii*."

By the way, Vincent, a design consultant who has been living in Japan for 20 years, wrote that the closest word to "*kawaii*" is "interesting" in English (Vincent 2014).

2.1.4 *"Kawaii" and its Derivatives*

"*Kawaii*" is an adjective and is written as "可愛い" in Japanese, which is a combination of the stem "可愛" and the suffix "い" to make the word to be an adjective.

The stem "可愛" consists of "可" and "愛" where the former is a prefix to mean "–able," "-ible," "possible," and "can" and the latter is a word meaning love and affection.

Following is a list of derivatives of "可愛."

"可愛い" (*Kawaii*) adj. pretty, sweet, cute, tiny, dear, darling

"可愛がる" (*Kawai-garu*) v.t. to love, to make a pet of, to be affectionate to a person.

"可愛げ" (*Kawai-ge*) n. the charm of an innocent child

"可愛さ" (*Kawai-sa*) n. the cuteness or the manner of being "可愛い"

"可愛らしい" (*Kawai-rashii*) adj. the appearance of being "可愛い"

"可愛らしさ" (*Kawai-rashisa*) n. noun form of "可愛らしい."

2.2   Historical Overview of *Kawaii* in Japan

2.2.1   Heian *Era (794–1185)*

This section describes the historical background of the *Kawaii* concept in Japan.

It is common to go back to Sei-shonagon as the first author who wrote about the concept of "*Kawaii*." Sei-shonagon was a writer and poet around 1000 AD/CE. Her most important work is an essay *Makura-(no)-Soushi* (枕草子). The famous part "pretty things (section 155)" is included in this chapter. It is partly translated by Waley (Shonagon 2011) as follows:

> The face of a child that has its teeth dug into a melon. A baby sparrow hopping towards one when one calls "chu, chu" to it; or being fed by its parents with worms or what not, when one has captured it and tied a thread to its foot. A child of three or so, that scurrying along suddenly catches sight of some small object lying on the ground, and clasping the thing in its pretty little fingers, brings it to show to some grown-up person. A little girl got up in cloister-fashion (bobbed hair) tossing back her head to get the hair away from her eyes because she wants to look at something.

In order to enable you to understand the visual image described in this text better, please consider Fig. 2.1. This image is a *manga* that Junko Shibata drew (Shibata 2016). The translation by Waley corresponds up to fifth frame of the

Fig. 2.1 Manga description of pretty things by Sei-Shonagon (Manga by Shibata J.; used with permission)

manga. Although the text in the *manga* is written in Japanese, you easily will be able to make a guess about what is being described.

The original title of this part is *Utukushiki-mono*, literally meaning "beautiful things," although Waley translated it as pretty things. The word *utukushi* at that time did not mean beautiful but the loving feeling of the viewer towards the infant or feeble person or small things. While "*utukushi*" meant pretty, as was explained, the origin of "*kawaii*" was "*kaho-hayushi*" at that time. "*Kaho*" means the face and "*hayushi*" means being embarrassed or ashamed.

In *Konjaku-Monogatari* (今昔物語) (Anonymous 1185, c. 12th century), which was edited in the twelfth century, there is a description in vol. 25, part 6 "この児に刀を突き立て, 矢を射立て殺さむは, なほかはゆし" meaning "Killing this boy by piercing with the sword and shooting the arrow is '*kahayushi* after all." This use of "*kahayushi*" has a meaning of being embarrassed or ashamed. This is also evidence that in Heian era "*Kahayushi*" does not have the meaning of cute nor pretty. The meaning was quite different from the word "*kawaii*" today.

"*Kaho-hayushi*" then became "*kahayushi*," then "*kawayui*" and "*kawaii*." As the notation of the word changes to "*kawaii*," its meaning also changed from an embarrassed feeling to a loving feeling and "*utukushi*" changed from a loving feeling to beautiful. "*Kawaisou*" came to have the meaning of an embarrassed feeling or pity. These transitions are summarized in Table 2.1.

Table 2.1 Word transition in Japanese regarding cute or pretty, beautiful and embarrassed feeling or pity

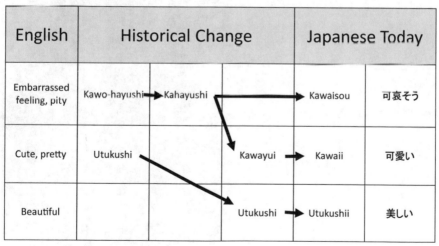

English	Historical Change			Japanese Today	
Embarrassed feeling, pity	Kawo-hayushi → Kahayushi			Kawaisou	可哀そう
Cute, pretty	Utukushi		Kawayui →	Kawaii	可愛い
Beautiful			Utukushi →	Utukushii	美しい

2.2.2   *After* Heian *Era and* Edo *Era (1603–1868)*

During the Heian era, when Sei-shonagon wrote her essay, Japan was governed by
the aristocracy and was rather peaceful. After the Heian era, those eras including
Kamakura (1185–1333), Muromachi (1336–1573) and Azuchi Momoyama (1573–
1603) followed, when the *samurai* fought each other and controlled each small land
area. We don't have clear evidence how the concept of "*kawaii*" was treated at that
time. In 1603, Ieyasu Tokugawa dominated all of Japan, and the Edo era started.
Although he was a *samurai*, the popular culture grew much in this era.

Endo (2014) wrote that one example of "*kawaii*" during that time is the *Maneki-
neko* or "a stylized image of a cat, with one paw raised in invitation, that serves as a
shopkeeper's charm for prosperity (Fig. 2.2)" (Collick et al. 2002). Endo hypoth-
esized that *Maneki-neko* was transformed from the fox statues as the messenger of
divinities that were placed at the gates of shrines (Fig. 2.3), of which a typical
example can be found at Fushimi Inari shrine in Kyoto and Anamori Inari shrine in
Tokyo. Though the body of fox is lean, the body and the paw of cat are round and
fat and look more "*kawaii*." At that time, cats were popular as a pet among
tradesmen and artisans.

Fig. 2.2 *Maneki-neko* (Photo
by Masaaki Kurosu, and used
with permission)

Fig. 2.3 Fox statue at
Anamori-inari shrine in
Tokyo (Photo by Masaaki
Kurosu, and used with
permission)

2.2.3 Meiji *Era (1868–1912) and* Taisho *Era (1912–1926)*

After the Edo era, the Meiji era followed, which was a time of great changes in
Japan, triggered by the arrival of Commodore Matthew Perry in 1853. At that time,
Japan opened her gates to foreign countries, imported knowledge and technology
from European countries, established the constitution and other social systems,
waged war against the Qing dynasty in China, Russia, *etc.* Perhaps Japanese people
did not have the time or calmness to enjoy the *kawaii* concept.

The next era was the *Taisho* era that began in 1912. Though the *Taisho* era lasted
only 15 years, many cultural movements collectively called "*Taisho* Roman"
occurred during that period.

Endo points that the "*Taisho* Roman" is influenced by the Japonism in European
countries that originally was influenced by Japanese culture in the Edo era. It is a
re-importation of the Japanese culture. Endo showed that the kewpie doll was
designed in 1909 by Rose O'Neill, who was an American illustrator influenced by
the Orientalism and the Japonism at that period. Kewpie is used as a mascot symbol
for mayonnaise by a Japanese company and is still popular in Japan. According to
her, such modern origin of *kawaii* examples like the kewpie doll is a result of
cultural mixture and is not just a pure-Japanese culture.

Another important movement occurred in 1914. Takarazuka Revue Company
was organized and held a revue. Takarazuka is an organization where only young
women play the role of men and women in a musical show. Fans of Takarazura
ranged from teenagers to seniors, most of which were women. It is a critical point
that women-culture had a focal point that leads to *kawaii* culture. *Kawaii* has a
deep-rooted preference among women until today.

2.2.4 Showa *Era (1926–1989)*

Regarding the *kawaii* concept, we cannot forget Nobuko Yoshiya (1896–1973) and the *Ribbon* magazine. Yoshiya was a Japanese novelist whose novels were loved by very many young women. Her novels dealt with friendship and love among women. Similar to Takarazuka, young women, especially before their marriage, paid attention to the way of life of other young women. This tendency served as the basis of *kawaii* culture today.

Ribbon is a *manga* magazine for young girls up to around 12–13 years old and started its publication in 1955. It is a separately bound magazine supplement that attracted young girls interested in *kawaii* things. The peak of its publication occurred from the late 1970s to the mid-1990s. The publication's contents included *manga* that described active love affairs among young girls and was called the "Bible of Young Girls."

Jun-ichi Nakahara (1913–1983) was a painter and a fashion designer. He drew beautiful young women with big eyes and designed modern dresses. His drawings influenced the fashion of young women at that time and still have a high reputation.

Yan (2010) analyzed these trends among young women and girls as a suspended period before marriage, which was the goal of a woman until the end of World War 2. After World War 2, girls' culture took a different form in such movements as a surrogating experience through the *manga* The Roses of Versailles by Riyoko Ikeda (1947–). Japanese girls projected their self-images into French aristocrats and expanded their dream world. On the other hand, there also were a stream of *Otome*-tic *manga* that were written, for example, by A-ko Mutsu (1954–). "*Otome*-tic" *manga* were not describing a dream world but rather the real world around young women, in which they have to commit themselves.

After *Ribbon*, there appeared many fashion magazines for teenagers and young women such as *An-an* that started in 1970 and *Non-no* that started in 1971. Recent trends of *kawaii* in relation to fashions, magazines, and other cultural factors will be discussed in Sect. 2.4.

2.3 The Popularity of *Kawaii*

2.3.1 Kawaii *is Now Flooding Japan*

One day, at a boutique in Tokyo, co-author Masaaki heard the following conversation:

> Mother: This coat is *kawaii* and will fit you well, won't it?
> Daughter: Oh how *kawaii* it is! But this one is also *kawaii*, isn't it?
> Mother: Hmm, indeed both are *kawaii*. But I can buy you just one of them. I think either will do, 'cause you're a *kawaii* girl.
> Daughter: I know, I know, I'm *kawaii* and will look nice with either one.

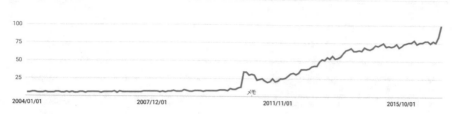

Fig. 2.4 Popularity of *kawaii* in Japan (Google Trends 2017.01.05)

The mother was around her mid-40s and the daughter seems to be around 18. In this case, the word "*kawaii*" is used frequently to describe both the object (coat) and the person (daughter). It was amazing that the word "*kawaii*" is repeated so many times as if the two people did not know other adjectives. They didn't mention the color, material, or design, but only the total impression of the coat by using the word "*kawaii.*" They did not talk about the face, style, sense of fashion, nor personality of the daughter, but only about the total impression of the daughter by a single word "*kawaii.*"

Today, *kawaii* is generic and is frequently used in many situations by many people especially among (young) women for describing beauty, attractiveness, and appeal as well as cuteness and prettiness. Its connotation is vast and seems to be quite situation-dependent, which will be discussed in Sect. 2.4.

How the word "*kawaii*" has been used in Japan is shown in Fig. 2.4. Google Trends show that the trend curve rising monotonically since 2010.

2.3.2 Kawaii *is also Trending in the World*

The Japan Expo started in France in 1999 based on the interest of *manga* and *animé* among French youth. The event attracts many European youth, especially young girls. The total attendance at the first Japan Expo that was held near Paris was 3200 in the site of 2500 m². However, in 2016, the total attendance grew to 250,000 at the 17th Expo. The size of the site was enlarged to 125,000 m². This event is now focusing on aspects of Japanese culture and pop culture and "*kawaii*" is one of the central concepts.

In 2007 the Ministry of Foreign Affairs of Japan created the International *Manga* Award, which attracted 245 entries from 38 countries. The ministry started the *Animé* Ambassador project in 2008. In 2009, as the Trend Communicators of Japanese Pop Culture, whose alias is *Kawaii* Ambassadors, three young female fashion models [Misako Aoki (1982–), Yuu Kimura (1986–), and Shizuka Fujioka (1989–)] were nominated to carry out publicity activities. In 2010, the METI (Ministry of Economy, Trade and Industry) started the office of Cool Japan.

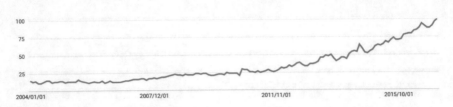

Fig. 2.5 Popularity of *kawaii* culture in the world (Google Trends 2017.01.05)

In addition to these official activities, the popularity of Hello Kitty and other cute characters such as *Tare*-Panda, *Monchhichi*, Astro-boy (*Tetsuwan* Atom), *Pikachu*, et al., attracted the hearts of foreign people. However, note that this development does not mean that foreign cute figures are not popular, even loved, in Japan. Japanese people also love Mickey Mouse, Miffy (*Nijntje*), Garfield, Sponge Bob, and other foreign-born characters. In any case, as shown in Fig. 2.5, the popularity of *kawaii* is a somewhat exponentially increasing in the world. According to Sakurai (2009), some foreign girls even want to become Japanese. This is the first time that Japanese culture is enthusiastically attracting attention among ordinary people in foreign countries.

Today, it is common to find *kawaii*-related shops in foreign countries. For example, there is a shop *Kawae* import (www.kawaeimport.se) in Uppsala, Sweden, where small decorated objects, stuffed dolls, and other Japanese items are sold as well as Lolita fashion goods. In other word, *kawaii* is now a synonym of Japanese culture.

However, this tendency should not be interpreted simply that the *kawaii* culture that originated in Japan has conquered the world. It could be said that some mental mechanism similar to the sympathy among foreign people was triggered by the Japanese *kawaii* culture. It would seem appropriate to say that the *kawaii* culture of Japan has become global because everyone in the world has something in common that resonates with a similar emotional mechanism. Abe (2015) wrote "*Kawaii* and child-likeness is now spreading throughout the world as a value that transcends the generation, social position, and region."

2.4 Three Types of *Kawaii*

In this section, we present a classification model of *kawaii*. The three models of *kawaii* proposed include: (1) Psycho-physical *kawaii*, (2) Cultural *kawaii*, and (3) Generic *kawaii*. In this classification, the current trend described in Sect. 3.2 will be described in terms of the cultural *kawaii* model.

Nittono (2016) proposed a two-layer model of *kawaii*. He wrote "*Kawaii* has two aspects: one is an aspect of feeling and another is an aspect of cultural value." What he categorized as *kawaii* as feeling is similar to our category of the psycho-physical *kawaii*, and what he categorized as cultural value is almost the same as our category of cultural *kawaii*. But there is another *kawaii* concept that should be called the generic *kawaii*, of which one can find an example in the conversation in Sect. 3.1 between the mother and daughter.

2.4.1   *Psycho-physical* Kawaii

Physical characteristics of objects, such as the shape, size, length, color, and texture, will affect the *kansei* of observers. Sometimes, *kansei* is simply described as the mixture of perception and emotion. However, one should not forget about the projection mechanism of the human observer. *Kawaii* is expressed as a property of an object and can be found in the expression "That baby animal is cute" or "This girl is pretty." On the other hand, emotion is what occurs *inside* the human being. Thus, such an expression as "I feel happy to see that baby animal" or "I love this girl" is possible, but one doesn't say "I feel *kawaii* to see that baby animal" or "I feel *kawaii* towards this girl." *Kawaii* is an impression "projected" onto the object based on the feeling of a person as if it is a property of the object itself. In other words, *kawaii* is not a feeling but is a *kansei* impression.

Psycho-physics is a discipline that studies the relationship between the physical characteristics of a stimulus and the resultant psychological impressions, sensations, or perceptions. An early approach in this direction in relation to cuteness is the ethological concept of baby schema (*Kindchenschema*) proposed by Lorenz (1943). This schema is a set of physical features including the big head compared to the whole body size, the round and protruding face, high forehead, big eyes, and small nose and mouth. These features are thought to be biologically provided so that they cause an affective response, and the baby consequently can receive much caretaking by adults. The same visual features can be found in *Makura-no-Soushi* (Fig. 2.1). The baby schema has a strong influence in academia even today [*e.g.*, Glocker (2009)].

With regard to the psycho-physical *kawaii* attributes, Ohkura (2016) conducted a series of psychological experiments in terms of shape, color, and texture instead of an organic stimulus, such as a baby's face. She first examined if there are *kawaii* shapes and *kawaii* colors, using colored figures including the square, circle, heart shape, star shape, *etc.*, in various colors. What she found was that round shapes are judged to be *kawaii* more than sharp shapes. She also found that pink, orange, yellow, and green are judged to be *kawaii* more than other colors, especially cold colors. Furthermore, she found that colors with high luminosity and high saturation are preferred to be *kawaii*. Regarding texture, she found that soft and fluffy materials are *kawaii*. These materials, also, have concordant onomatopoeia expressions, such as *fusa-fusa*, *mof-mof*, *fuka-fuka*, *mosa-mosa*, and *pof-pof*. On the contrary, materials with such associated onomatopoeia expressions, such as "*zak-zak*," "*jogi-jogi*," "*jusa-jusa*," "*jori-jori*," "*goro-goro*," and "*zag-zag*" are not *kawaii*. The size of objects was also found to relate with *kawaii*: smaller objects are judged to be *kawaii* more than larger objects. However, she found, also, that very tiny objects are not necessarily judged to be *kawaii*. There seemed to be an optimum range of size in relation to *kawaii*.

Regarding the size of objects, O-Young (1982), a Korean researcher of comparative culture, who does not explicitly discuss the issue of *kawaii*, but has pointed out the core characteristics of Japanese culture, wrote that there is a special prefix *mame* meaning "beans" in the Japanese language. The prefix "*mame*" is used when something is very tiny (and *kawaii*) in the situation such as "*mame-hon*" (tiny book), "*mame-jidousha*" (tiny automobile, including both real and toy vehicles), "*mame-ningyo*" (tiny doll), and "*mame-denkyu*" (tiny light bulb). This tendency is still viable, so as to produce the strap ornament for cell phones. In the case of a lunch pack, Japanese culture invented *orizume-bento* (a lunch packed in a small box). A famous rock garden at Ryoan-ji in Kyoto is also a miniature of the whole universe. Bonsai is a small-sized tree by which people can enjoy nature in a small flower pot. All of these examples, O-Young insists, are representing the tendency of Japanese people towards miniaturization, or shrinkage.

Today, Sylvanian Families doll house manufactured by Epoch Co., Ltd., is also a *kawaii* example of shrinkage. *Puri-kura*, or a photo-sticker booth that first appeared in 1995 in Japan, is similar to the photo booth that can be found in many countries to take passport pictures. However, because of the small size of the pictures, with many decorations, it is now an example of pop culture in Japan. Hence, it could be said that there are many typical examples of small items in Japan that trigger the *kawaii* impression.

As a summary of this subsection, the baby schema by Lorenz is an instinctive tendency that is prevalent among mammals. Ohkura found that such psycho-physical dimensions as color, shape, and texture as well as size are related to *kawaii*. Furthermore, O-Young proposed that small size is one of the major cultural features of Japan. Regarding the cultural *kawaii*, this topic will be discussed more in detail in Sect. 4.2.

Although this topic is not a fashion trend, this psycho-physical *kawaii* can be accepted by almost all people, including both male and female, from young to old, as shown in Fig. 2.6. Note that the ordinate is the rough estimated population and is not showing the exact number because the statistical data regarding such characteristics has not yet been released.

2.4.2 *Cultural* Kawaii

Regarding the cultural *kawaii* in Japan, there are at least two types of young women and girls including Lolita and Gal.

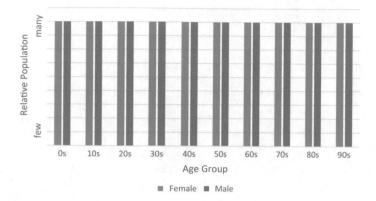

Fig. 2.6 Psycho-physical *kawaii* can be accepted by almost all the people

2.4.2.1 Lolita

First, the relationship between Lolita and *Loli* should be explained. *Loli* is a typical Japanese short form constructed for Lolita, which is related to the novel by Nabokov (1955). In the novel, the leading character Humbert has a pedophilic desire for and is strongly attracted by 12-year-old Lolita (Dolores Haze). Based on the novel, the term Lolita complex was generated in Japan. Lewis Carroll, who had a collection of photographs of Alice Liddell and other young girls, is said to be an example of someone who had a Lolita complex. It is called *Loli-con* in short, and the word "*Loli*" has become to have a meaning of attractive young girl. In the novel, Lolita was a sexual attraction, and the *Loli-con* tendency is still found today in *manga*, especially those sold at *Comiket* (comic market).

However, the Japanese Lolita fashion movement is different from *Loli-con* and is *not* targeting men. Only the connotation of the attractiveness of a young girl is common between Lolita fashion and *Loli-con*. Lolita fashion is the movement among young girls for themselves and has almost no sexual connotation. Young girls in Lolita fashion do not care for the eyes of men. In this sense, Lolita fashion has something in common with *Takarazuka*, the novel of Nobuko Yoshiya and paintings by Jun-ichi Nakahara.

Lolita fashion is typically described in the novel *Shimotsuma Monogatari* by Takemoto (2002). In this novel, the heroine Momoko Ryugasaki is a high-school student who lives in a rural town near Tokyo. She wears Lolita fashion for her own satisfaction. Her fashion style is quite different from that of her classmates and neighbors, but she does not mind it at all. She is going her own way by herself. This strong self-contained tendency is the main characteristic of Momoko. She is strong and independent, although dependent on her father financially. In other words, Lolita fashion is not limited to the costume, makeup, nail art, and hair style; it is the entire mental orientation aiming at self-satisfaction.

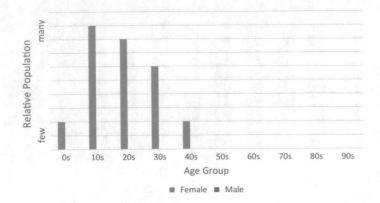

Fig. 2.7 The Lolita fashion is a trend for girls and young women

The characteristics of Lolita fashion include dressing in baroque, rococo, or Victorian style, complete with ribbon, lace, and frills. Inside the skirt, Lolita girls wear the *pannier*, or hoop petticoat, in order to make the clothing bulge outward. Preferred colors are white, pink, and other off-white colors. They carry a *pochette*, or small handbag, and such small decoration items as a flower, fruit, animal, sweets, heart, coronet, *etc*.

Lolita fashion is the *kawaii* movement among girls and young women. See Fig. 2.7, in which the ordinate is a rough estimate, and the total population of those who wear Lolita fashion is not yet clear. However, the figure shows that the Lolita fashion trend o is only among females.

An example of Lolita fashion can be seen in Fig. 2.8. These girls typically can be found in the Harajuku area of Tokyo.

Historically, Lolita fashion started in the 1970s when the boutique MILK opened in Harajuku. After that, many boutiques opened such as "BABY, THE STARS SHINE BRIGHT, Angelic Pretty, and Jane Marple. Then, many different concepts were created such as *Ama-Loli* (Sweet Lolita) and Classical Lolita (Fig. 2.9).

In 1990s, goth-*Loli* or gothic and Lolita, was born under the influence of the fashion of Vivienne Westwood and of "visual rock bands," such as X Japan and Buck-Tick. The Goth-*Loli* fashion features lace, ribbon, and frills in black or white. Preferred colors include black, white, pink, purple, and blue (Fig. 2.10). Goth-Loli is sometimes also called "visual, which comes from the visual rock band style.

2.4.2.2 Gal or *Garu*

Gal means a young girl or woman with unique makeup and fashion whose central area is Shibuya in Tokyo, which is located 1.6 km from Harajuku. Typically, these young girls or women dye their hair gold or brown, put on white loose socks (loose is pronounced "looze" in this case) with short skirt, and put on striking makeup (Fig. 2.11).

Fig. 2.8 Example of Lolita fashion (*Illustration* Thitiporn Yaisemsen and used with permission)

Fig. 2.9 Ama-Loli and classical Lolita (*Illustration* Pandita Watanachariya, and used with permission)

Fig. 2.10 Goth-Loli fashion (*Illustration* Thitiporn Yaisemsen and Pandita Watanachariya, and used with permission)

Fig. 2.11 Typical gal (*Illustration* Pandita Watanachariya and used with permission)

The core generation of gal fashion is JK (*"Joshi-Kousei"* meaning high-school girls) to whom singers Namie Amuro (1977–) and Ayumi Hamasaki (1978–) are charismatic symbols. Unlike Lolita, gal fashion attracts young men, and it is not a trend of girls for themselves. The word *"kawaii"* fits more to Lolita, but gal can also be called *kawaii* as a different flow of fashion.

There are different types of gal fashion. In 1990s, typical behaviors among young women of around 20 years old or higher startled the world with such behavior as smoking in public, reading tabloids in trains, drinking at *izakaya*, enjoying *pachinko* (Japanese-style pinball machines using small metal balls played in noisy game parlors usually inhabited by men), *etc.*, that have been typical behavioral patterns for men in their 40s and 50s. The new word *oyaji*-gal was born in comics by Yutsuko Chusonji (1962–2005) to describe these young women. But *oyaji* gal women were not recognized as *kawaii*.

Contrary to *oyaji* gal, *ko*-gal, a new type of gal fashion, was born. *Ko* means small or young, and *ko*-gal girls were mainly high-school students and junior-high students. These girls changed their school uniform to "Gal" fashion sometimes in public restrooms and were seen gathering around entertainment zones of the city.

At the end of 1990s, *yamamba* fashion appeared, with girls who tanned their faces to brown (it is called *ganguro* meaning "dark face") and bleached their hair. Eye makeup with wide white eyeliner was another feature.

Hime-gal (princess girl) is another type of gal that appeared in the mid-2000s. They are also called age-*jou* (*ageha* ladies), because they are influenced by the magazine *Koakuma-Ageh*a (a little devil women). This magazine features young women working at *kyaba-kra* (cabaret clubs) who serve alcoholic beverages to men and chat with them. One of the prominent features of this fashion is *mori-gami* (enlarged hair at the top of the head).

In short, gal is a fashion trend among girls and young women whose fashion and makeup are unique, and the central location of this fashion is Shibuya. Gal-fashion fans, of course, do this for their own satisfaction, but many of the gal followers enjoyed playing with men. The range of age group is a bit narrow compared to Lolita fashion, including young women as well as girls, as shown in Fig. 2.12.

2.4.3 Generic Kawaii

Generic *kawaii* is a tendency that is characteristic among most women and some men (Fig. 2.13). The fashion described in Fig. 2.13 is not that of Lolita nor of gal. This kind of fashion can be found more frequently than the Lolita and gal fashion. It is not culturally specific among Japanese girls and young women, but is accepted by many of them as their daily *kawaii* fashion.

Most frequently, the word *"kawaii"* is similar to attractive, beautiful, lovable, matching, distinctive, unique, and other adjectives. If someone wishes to describe the fashion, makeup, personality, and other characteristics of a person, *kawaii* is a safe term that will not trigger unpleasantness. In an extreme case, even when one

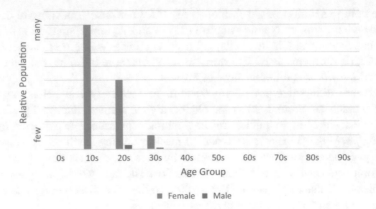

Fig. 2.12 Gal fashion is a trend among girls and young women

Fig. 2.13 Typical generic
kawaii (*Illustration* Pandita
Watanachariya and used with
permission)

sees a baby who does not look cute, the expression "Oh, your baby is *kawaii*!
(because it is a baby)" is used.

This type of *kawaii* is somewhat related to the psycho-physical *kawaii*, especially in the case of babies and small accessories. However, regarding the generic
kawaii, there are many exceptions. For example, the size of the object should not
always be small. Character costumes such as Funassy and *Kumamon*, which are
called *yuru-chara* (loose character) and are large-sized because there is a person

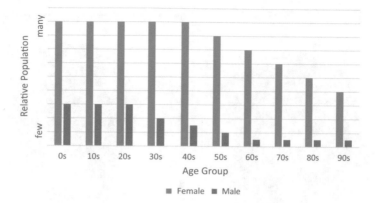

Fig. 2.14 Generic *kawaii* can be found among most women and some men in Japan

inside the costume, are regarded as *kawaii*. These are the generic *kawaii* type. In addition, grown-ups can be called *kawaii,* and it is not unusual to say, "This old man/woman is *kawaii*." Furthermore, some men can be described as *kawaii* especially when they are young. These trends are expressed in Fig. 2.14. Note that, again, the chart is showing just a rough estimate and is not based on any statistical survey.

2.4.4 Other Types of **Kawaii**

"*Kawaii*" as used in Japanese culture, has generated many variations as follows.

2.4.4.1 *Yume-Kawaii*

Yume-kawaii (Fig. 2.15) is a fashion term that means a dream-like *kawaii* and is close to the concept of Lolita (Fig. 2.9). Colors used for this fashion are not strong or vivid but pastel colors, which are pale, light, and soft. Preferred visual themes include clouds, insects, stars, unicorns, *etc*. Because this is a fashion trend, some Lolita girls and women wear a dress with these visual themes.

2.4.4.2 *Kimo-Kawaii*

Kimo-kawaii is a concept that is eerie or creepy. At the same time, *kimo-kawaii* has something *kawaii*, as can be seen in Fig. 2.16. This is not a clothing fashion style, and no one wears this kind of fashion. This is a style applied to objects, including

Fig. 2.15 *Yume-kawaii* examples (*Illustration* Thitiporn Yaisemsen, and used with permission)

Fig. 2.16 *Kimo-kawaii* examples (*Illustration* Thitiporn Yaisemsen, and used with permission)

dolls and illustration. However, sometimes, an entertainer whose atmosphere is somewhat creepy is called *Kimo-Kawaii*.

2.4.4.3   *Gro-Kawaii*

Gro-kawaii is a concept that is similar to *kimo-kawaii*. As can be seen in Fig. 2.17, *gro-kawaii* is much more grotesque and is related to sadism more than the creepiness of *kimo-kawaii*, but it is still is a bit *kawaii*.

2.4.4.4   *Ero-Kawaii*

Ero-kawaii is a combination of eroticism and *kawaii* as shown in Fig. 2.18. Because images of *ero-kawaii* are half-naked, *ero-kawaii* girls and women cannot be frequently seen on the street but can be found in magazines, photographs, and movies.

2.4.4.5   *Busu-Kawaii*

Busu-kawaii is applied to girls and women who are ugly, "fugly" (extremely ugly), or unattractive, but are somewhat *kawaii* (Fig. 2.19). This is not a fashion style but is an overall description by men of a girl or woman.

Fig. 2.17   *Gro-kawaii* examples (*Illustration* Thitiporn Yaisemsen, and used with permission)

Fig. 2.18 *Ero-Kawaii* examples (*Illustration* Thitiporn Yaisemsen, and used with permission)

Fig. 2.19 *Busu-kawaii* examples (*Illustration* Thitiporn Yaisemsen, and used with permission)

2.5 *Kawaii* **Culture Today**

2.5.1 *Related Concepts*

In this subsection, we explain several concepts that are related to *kawaii*.

2.5.1.1 *Moe* (萌え)

Moe (萌え)" originated in such subcultures as *animé*, *manga*, and game software around the 1990s and is now used in wider contexts. "*Moe*" means having a strong preference or favor. As a result, "*Moe*" represents a positive feeling or attachment. *Suki* (好き) means a general sense of preference and "*Moe*" means a stronger sense of preference. "*Moe*" is narrower and deeper than the general term "*Suki*." The origin of "*Moe*" is a description of plants growing from a seed, thus implying the rise of strong feelings.

Sometimes *moe* has a sexual connotation. For example, young *kawaii* girls wearing the school uniform or the shop-assistant uniform gives rise to pedophilic *moe* feelings.

2.5.1.2 *Otaku* (おたく)

Otaku (おたく) is a lover of pop culture and sub-cultures including *manga*, *animé*, sci-fi, games, pop idols, Internet, train models, dolls, *etc*. The term is similar to the English word geek or nerd, but does not completely match to either of them. Many *otaku* boys and men (and sometimes girls and women) can be found in Akihabara, Tokyo, where electronics are sold. They usually have some obsessive feeling for the target item or concept. *Moe* is one of the characteristic feelings among *otaku* people. As a result, *otaku* people love *kawaii* but in a somewhat different sense from that of Lolita people.

2.5.1.3 *Meido* (メイド)

"*Meido*" (メイド) comes from the English word "maid." However, among *otaku*, it means young waitresses of *cafés* or restaurants who wear a uniform, especially an apron dress. In Akihabara and other area, there are *meido*-cafés where many meido girls can be found. The term refers to a kind of attachment to girls or women in uniforms.

2.5.1.4 Sailor *Fuku* (セーラー服)

Sailor *fuku* (セーラー服) is the typical school uniform for young girls at junior high schools and high schools. It literally means a sailor suit, but actually is the uniform for girls, because the middy blouse and skirt in dark blue color with white stripes looks like a sailor's uniform.

Sailor *fuku* is preferred by girls themselves as well as *Otaku*. Girls think it to be *kawaii*. However, sometimes girls regard the style as a symbol of the restraint in school and society, and they change their uniforms to more casual fashions. On the other hand, *Otaku* guys love the style, because of a fetish feeling towards the uniform in a similar way to *Meido*.

2.5.1.5 *Cosplay* (コスプレ)

Cosplay (コスプレ) is a shortened Japanese form of "costume play" in which people wear the dress or uniform of a hero or heroine of *animé* or games to disguise themselves. The motivation of those who do *cosplay* is to have fun by identifying themselves with the hero or heroine. A wider meaning of *cosplay* includes those who wear the uniform of *meido* or sailor *fuku*, although they are not really working as a maid or are not really school girls. Many *cosplay* people can be found in *Comiket*, or the comic market, which is held twice each year in Tokyo.

2.5.2 *Desire to be* Kawaii

In relation to the fact that *kawaii* mainly refers to female culture, the result of a survey conducted by Yomoda (2006) as shown in Fig. 2.20 is interesting. He conducted a questionnaire survey about *kawaii* with a total of 245 Japanese university students (89 male and 156 female), for whom the ages ranged from 18 to 23. One of the results shown is that those who want to be called *kawaii* are 68% female and only 26% male. Notably, informants aged 18 wanting to be called *kawaii* were 78% female and only 15% male. These results show that *kawaii* is a gender-specific cultural concept, and females tend to become *kawaii* for themselves, while males tend to love *kawaii* (girls and women).

2.5.3 Kawaii *and Beautiful*

In western countries, it is said that beauty is generally more important and valuable than cuteness or prettiness for girls and women. Yomoda (2006) wrote of an episode in which he was warned not to use the word "cute" to a woman (not to a small child). The female editor of a magazine told him that the use of "cute" for a

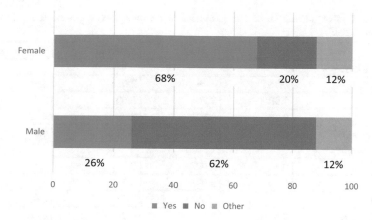

Fig. 2.20 The chart shows the proportion of answers to the question "Do you want to be called *kawaii*?" [Adapted from the data of Yomoda (2006)]

woman may be regarded as a discrimination from the viewpoint of political correctness. In other words, cuteness is valuable only for children.

However, in Japan, as shown in Figs. 2.7 and 2.12, it seems that girls and young women put more emphasis on *kawaii* than beauty. The age that Japanese women start using the word beauty is after they have graduated from the age of using *kawaii*, roughly speaking after their 20s.

For confirming this hypothesis, a small-sized questionnaire research was conducted by coauthor Masaaki using 228 photographs including female actors, *animé* characters, animals, entertainers, *etc.* (Kurosu and Hashizume 2016) A total of 89 university students (55 male and 34 female) participated as informants. They were presented with photographs one-by-one and were asked if they know the person, character, or object (by answering 0 or 1) and to rate the degree of *kawaii*, beauty, and preference on a five-point rating scale.

Table 2.2 shows part of the results of the questionnaire research survey described in (Kurosu and Hashizume 2016). The column "Know" is an average of "don't know it" as 0 and "know it" as 1, Three other columns, *Kawaii*, Beautiful, and Preference show the average rating score for the five-point scale. The lowest row is the result of *T*-test (*p* value) between male informants and female informants. Pale yellow cells means the *p* value was lower than or equal to 0.01.

The result for Mickey Mouse is easy to understand. Female students preferred Mickey more than male students and rated it as *kawaii* for 4.32, while beautiful for 2.98. The result for the flower (Peony) is also reasonable. Informants gave higher ratings for beautiful than *kawaii*.

The result for human paintings and human photographs are interesting. While informants gave very high ratings of 4.03 for Mona Lisa on beauty, they gave low rating of 1.83 on *kawaii* on average. It is easy to understand considering the generally accepted recognition that Mona Lisa is one of the most beautiful paintings in the world. However, in terms of actresses, including Marilyn Monroe, Audrey

Table 2.2 Part of the results of the questionnaire research survey described in Kurosu and Hashizume (2016)

	Know	Kawaii	Beautiful	Preference
Mickey Mouse				
Total	0.94	4.29	2.91	4.09
Male	0.90	3.70	2.60	3.50
Female	0.98	4.32	2.98	4.32
T-test (*p* value)	0.59	0.07	0.72	0.09
Flower (Peony)				
Total	0.31	3.07	3.72	3.18
Male	0.29	3.07	3.73	3.25
Female	0.35	3.00	3.71	3.06
T-test (*p* value)	0.55	0.95	0.94	0.46
Mona Lisa				
Total	0.97	1.83	4.03	2.76
Male	0.90	1.80	4.00	3.00
Female	1.00	1.84	4.04	2.67
T-test (*p* value)	0.34	0.91	0.93	0.40
Marilyn Monroe				
Total	0.80	3.00	3.96	3.30
Male	0.82	2.89	*3.71*	3.11
Female	0.76	3.18	*4.35*	3.59
T-test (*p* value)	0.56	0.24	*0.01*	0.08
Audrey Hepburn				
Total	0.39	3.53	3.97	3.43
Male	*0.25*	*3.24*	*3.67*	*3.18*
Female	*0.62*	*4.00*	*4.44*	*3.82*
T-test (*p* value)	*0.00*	*0.00*	*0.00*	*0.00*
Scarlett Johansson				
Total	0.19	3.13	3.87	3.26
Male	0.22	3.20	3.78	3.33
Female	0.15	3.03	4.00	3.15
T-test (*p* value)	0.40	0.46	0.40	0.40

Hepburn, and Scarlett Johansson, the *kawaii* scores rise up almost to the level of beautiful (although beautiful scores a bit higher than *kawaii*). Japanese university students regarded these actresses as *kawaii* as well as beautiful.

These results suggest the necessity for future comparative studies in different countries and cultures. The result of the comparative studies may show us the differences (or similarities) of *kawaii*-related concepts in Japan and other countries. It may lead to the conclusion that *kawaii* cannot simply be translated as cute or pretty or *mignon* (French) or *carina* (Italian).

2.5.4 Kawaii *and Horror*

Sometimes, something that was designed to look *kawaii* and to be loved by young girls provokes a horrifying feeling. A doll is a typical example. Kawaii dolls in Fig. 2.21 may trigger the sensation of fear depending on the viewer's psychological condition and the context. There are many movies in Japan and foreign countries that focus on the horror of dolls [examples include *Tourist Trap* (1979), *Child's Play* (1988), *Dolls* (1987), Hanako-san *in the Toilet* (2003), *The Doll Maste*r (2005), *etc.*].

The psychological mechanism is not yet clear but the hypothesis of Uncanny Valley proposed by Mori (1970) may explain this phenomenon. His hypothesis is not about the doll but about the humanoid robot. However, the basic mechanism of Uncanny Valley may be applied to dolls. The basic point of his hypothesis is this: as the humanoid becomes more human-like, it will be positively accepted by human beings. However, when its similarity to the human becomes higher, it will be perceived as uncanny. In any case, this theme needs to be analyzed further to clarify the relationship between *kawaii* and horror.

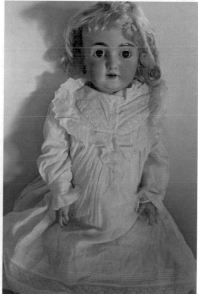

Fig. 2.21 Japanese antique doll and German antique bisque doll (*Photo* Masaaki Kurosu, owned by Masaaki Kurosu.)

2.6   Conclusion

In this chapter, we have discussed *kawaii* in Japan from many different perspectives. *Kawaii* culture that has its own historical origins far back in the tenth century is now widely accepted throughout the world. There is a possibility that *kawaii* sensitivity is universal, and Japan has simply been the first to exploit it. However, *kawaii* is not completely identical with such foreign concepts as cute, pretty, *mignon* and *carina*. It is not yet clear that the Japanese *kawaii* concept is accepted by foreigners based on a proper understanding of the core concept. It is likely that only the surface layer of culture is acknowledged, accepted, and assimilated outside of Japan.

We have distinguished three differen *kawaii* concepts. First is the psychophysical *kawaii*, which must be common among all human beings, because it is based on an instinctive sensitivity. Second is the cultural *kawaii*. What is now prevalent in the world is this type of *kawaii*. In this context, two types of *kawaii* girls and young women, *i.e.*, Lolita and Gal, are clarified. It is the culture of girls and young women for themselves and by themselves. The third type is the generic *kawai*i, for which most women and some men use the term *kawaii* in their everyday life. This type of *kawaii* is generic, because the word is used in different situations that could be described by other words such as attractive, beautiful, notable, *etc.*, as well as cute or pretty.

Finally, we discussed some related words and the attitudes of males and females to the concept of *kawaii*. Based on the result of the questionnaire research, Japanese tend to describe actresses as *kawaii* at almost the same level of beauty.

Further studies should be conducted to clarify the concept of *kawaii* from such social sciences as psychology, sociology, anthropology, and *kansei* engineering.

References

Abe K (2015) Childishness as a strategy—storytelling manner of *"Kawaii"* and maturity (in Japanese). Asahi-sensho 938, Asahi-Shinbunsha
Anonymous (around 12th century) (1185) Konjaku Monogatari
Collick M, Dutcher DP, Tanabe S, Kaneko M (2002) Kenkyusha's New College Japanese-English Dictionary, 5th edn., Kenkyusha
Endo K (2014) Philosophy of *"Kawaii"* at the intersection of globalization and localization (in Japanese), 5th Synthetic Symposium of Transdisciplinary Federation of Science and Technology
Glocker ML, Langleben DD, Ruparel K, Loughead JW, Gur RC, Sachser N (2009) Baby schema in infant faces induces cuteness perception and motivation for caretaking in adults. Ethology 115(3):257–263
Johnson S (1755) A dictionary of the english language (Reprinted by Yushodo, Tokyo 1983)
Kurosu M, Hashizume A (2016) On the concept of *Kawaii* (in Japanese). SIG Kansei, Japan Society for Kansei Engineering
Lorenz K (1943) Die angeborenen Formen moeglicher Erfahrung. Z Tierpsychol 5:235–409

Mori M (1970) The Uncanny Valley (in Japanese). Energy 7(4):33–35 (English translation at http://spectrum.ieee.org/automaton/robotics/humanoids/the-uncanny-valley. 29 Jan 2017

Nabokov V (1955) Lolita. The Olympia Press

Nichols B, Pickett JP, Kleinedler SR, Leonesio C (2011) The American Heritage Dictionary of the English Language, 5th edn., Houghton Mifflin Harcourt

Nittono H (2016) A Psychological model of 'Kawaii' feeling (in Japanese). Info Process 57(2):128–131

O-Young L (1982) Japanese people aiming at the Shrinkage (in Japanese), Gakusei-sha

Ohkura M (2016) Systematic research of Kawaii Artifacts—Physical Attributes of Artifacts that have the Kansei value of 'Kawaii' (in Japanese). Info Process 57(2):124–127

Oxford English Dictionary (2010) http://www.oed.com/.www.oed.com/

Sakurai T (2009). World Kawaii Evolution—why do they cry "We Want to Be Japanese"? (in Japanese), PHP Shinsho

Shonagon S (around 1000) "Makura-no-Soushi" (translated by Waley, A. (2011) The Pillow Book of Sei Shonagon. Tuttle Publishing)

Shibata J (2016) High School Old Japanese Literature—Such Stories You're Reading (in Japanese), KST Production

Takebayashi S, Azuma N (2003). Kenkyusha's New English-Japanese Dictionary, 7th edn., Kenkyusha

Takemoto N (2002) "Kamikaze Girls (Shimotsuma Monogatari) (in Japanese). Shogakukan

Vincent T (2014) "Kawaii Japan", PEN, No. 368, p 98

Yan X (2010) Generation and transformation of 'Kawaii' concept in modern society (in Japanese), Hyogo University of Teacher Education, Graduate School of Education Master's Thesis #09141F

Yomoda I (2006) On Kawaii (in Japanese) Chikuma Shinsho 578, Chikuma-Shobo

Chapter 3
Cuteness in China

Cuteness in Chinese is written as 可爱 (kě ài), which literally means "worth lov-ing." In this chapter, we first review the evolution of the meaning of cuteness in Chinese literature. Then, we present the conventional Chinese style of cuteness in visual design, followed by the three movements (*i.e.*, *Kawaii* culture, *Moe* culture, and *Baozou* phenomenon) that have reshaped how Chinese people perceive cute-ness currently. After that, we discuss the general development of Chinese cuteness industry, and we use a successful case study to demonstrate how cuteness design may thrive as a business that bridges culture and technology in China.

3.1 Evolution of the Meaning of Cuteness in Chinese Literature

The term *kě ài* has two major senses in ancient and modern Chinese. The first sense is "respectable," *i.e.*, someone/something being respected and beloved. The earliest records of such usage date back to the Han dynasty. For example, it is said in *The Book of Documents* (《尚书》,《虞书·大禹谟》chapter), one of the Five Classics (五经) of ancient Chinese literature, that "可爱非君?可畏非民?" It means that the monarch should be respected (by the general public) while the common people should be feared (by the monarch). This term is also found in poems and essays in the Song and Ming dynasties, describing the magnificence of rocks (*e.g.*, 宋·陆游《老学庵笔记》"见荆棘中有崖石…奇古可爱"), trees (*e.g.*, 明·刘基《浣溪沙·秋思》词 "枫叶有霜缤可爱"), and flowers (*e.g.*, 宋·周敦颐的《爱莲说》"水陆草木之花,可爱者甚蕃"). In these words, the sense of respectable usually arises from something that is spectacularly big or dramatic. This usage is rarely found in Chinese today.

© Springer International Publishing AG 2017
A. Marcus et al., *Cuteness Engineering*, Springer Series on Cultural Computing,
DOI 10.1007/978-3-319-61961-3_3

The second sense is to denote someone/something being lovely, *i.e.*, lovable or adorable. There are also two scenarios in which cuteness in this sense was used in Chinese literature. One is to describe pretty girls. For example, Xi Zuochi, a historian in the Dong Jin Dynasty wrote in a letter to the King of Yan, "Hun people call their wives 'Yan Zhi', meaning that they are adorable as '*Yan Zhi*' (*i.e.*, rouge)" (东晋·习凿齿与燕王书曰:"匈奴名妻作'阏支',言其可爱如烟肢也。"). Shen Fu, a famous writer in the Qing Dynasty wrote in his book that a girl named Li Shiyuan looks as lovable as a fairy (清·沈复《浮生六记·闺房记乐》:"李诗宛如姑射仙子,有一种落花流水之趣,令人可爱。").

In the other scenario, the word cute is the synonym of delicate and vulnerable, especially when referring to children and small animals. For instance, Ouyang Xiu, a well-known writer in the Song Dynasty said in one of his poems that the oriole bird is as cute as a delicate baby, given its color and chirping sound (宋欧阳修《啼鸟》诗:"黄鹂颜色已可爱,舌端哑咤如娇婴。"). Such usage is more dominate in the Chinese language as suggested by the Chinese idioms. The word "cute" is often used in pair with words such as "naïve" (天真可爱), "lively" (活泼可爱), and "innocent" (稚气可爱) in description of young children. This usage is also reflected in the traditional Chinese style of visual designs.

3.2 Evolution of the Perception of Cuteness in Chinese Culture

In this section, we review how Chinese people adapt their perception of cuteness in visual designs, under the integrated influence of Chinese traditions, culture imports from East Asia and the West, as well as the undergoing social–economic changes in China.

3.2.1 Lovely in Traditional Chinese Culture

The illustration of cuteness in traditional Chinese artworks is often associated with children and animals. For instance, the baby/child characters (Fig. 3.1) in the Chinese New Year paintings, which express good wishes via depiction of scenes from folk stories, myths, and legends, are usually deemed to be cute. These characters tend to have a round face, a big head, and a fat body illustrated by smooth lines with few sharp angles. Such an image matches Chinese people's general view of adorable features of a baby in reality.

東洋綺談 TouyouKidan, Copyright © Tojo Miho

Fig. 3.1 Examples of traditional style of Chinese cuteness from Manga109 dataset (used with permission)

3.2.2   Kawaii *Culture*

In the 1980s and 1990s, the *kawaii* culture (卡哇伊 in Chinese) from Japan arrived in China through imported animations and *manga* such as Doraemon. Around the same time, the Disney Mickey Mouse and Friends became popular via TV programs. Since then, more and more cuteness franchises from abroad successfully entered the Chinese market and became fads among children and young adults. Besides Hello Kitty, which was named by Japan's tourism ministry as the goodwill tourism ambassador in China and Hong Kong in May 2008, other examples include Pikachu created by the Pokémon Company in Japan, Mashimaro[1] or 流氓兔 ("Hoodlum rabbit") in Chinese—a fictional character who resembles a fat rabbit from Korea, and Stitch from another Disney animation. After becoming exposed to a large variety of toys and accessories made with these characters or designs in a similar style (*e.g.*, Figs. 3.2, 3.3), Chinese people quickly adopted the idea of *kawaii*, which conveys the same set of cute features to which they are accustomed (*e.g.*, round face, big head, and fat body) in a more visually exaggerated manner.

Note that Chinese people's impression of *kawaii* is somewhat different from that in Japan. The meaning of *kawaii* is much narrower in China than in its birthplace. An informal survey (by co-author Ma based on several current blogs) has shown that about 90% of the Chinese people think that only something small, even tiny, and girls can be called *kawaii*. The term is also considered to be used primarily by females.

---

[1]https://en.wikipedia.org/wiki/Mashimaro.

Fig. 3.2 Example of cute
merchandise in the Chinese
market from the US (photo by
Xiaojuan Ma, and used with
permission)

Fig. 3.3 Examples of *kawaii*
products in the Chinese
market imported from Japan,
Korea, and the US (photo by
Xiaojuan Ma, and used with
permission)

3.2.3 Moe *Culture*

The concept of *moe* (萌 in Chinese) became a popular culture phenomenon in Japan
around the year 2003. Soon after, the wave spread to China through Japanese
animés, comics (*manga*), and video games (animated computer graphics or ACG).
At first a special expression circulated largely among Chinese ACG fans, since the
late 2000s, the term is used by the general public.

Moe is initially a slang term for describing a (female) character in ACG who can
evoke a feeling of strong affection (Fig. 3.4). At the time, the *moe* style of cuteness
mainly refers to sweet, vulnerable, innocent, somewhat naïve girls. Hence, unlike
kawaii, more males (the major body of ACG fans) adopted the idea of *moe* at the
beginning in China. As the diversity of properties of ACG characters adored by fans
increases, the meaning and usage of *moe* has been broadened to accommodate the
new types of cuteness (see the cuteness taxonomy chapter for more details). Later,
people find that such properties can be mapped to individuals in real life, and then
the term *moe* transforms from a subcultural slang to everyday language in China.

Fig. 3.4 Examples of *moe* souvenirs from Japanese ACG (photo by Jianqi Ma and Fengyuan Zhu, and used with permission)

3.2.4 Baozou *(Rage) Comic Phenomenon*

On October 1, 2015, the city police of Nanjing, China published a set of anti-fraud booklets in a *Baozou* comic (*i.e.*, rage comics in China)[2] style on its Weibo[3] and WeChat[4] account. In just one day, the booklets received over 200,000 clicks online. Many news media, including the CCTV (China Central Television) news Website, reported the success of this campaign (No Author 2015a). In the same month, the Weibo account of the official Taobao Store of the Forbidden City Museum[5] posted an article titled "Enough, Leave me Alone" (Fig. 3.5). The article told the story of the last emperor of the Ming Dynasty with *Baozou* comics (No Author 2015b). The purpose was to advertise the museum's lucky souvenirs. Over 1.27 million people have read the post and many left a "like."

These events have demonstrated the well-recognized ability of *Baozou* comics to evoke public attention in China, regardless of the heated debates on the appropriateness of using this new style of visual communication in scenarios that are often considered to be formal or serious. Compared to stylish graphics carefully designed by professionals, *Baozou* comics are unpolished, rough, ugly (in the conventional sense) sketches or images made usually by amateurs exploiting materials available on the Internet (see example in Fig. 3.5). In other words, they represent a type of "cuteness with negative properties" very different from the *kawaii* or *moe* style of cuteness (see the Cuteness Taxonomy Chapter for more details). However, despite its "minimal effort" aesthetic (Douglas 2014) and potential legal issues (Schiphorst 2013) as a type of Internet meme, *Baozou* comics have rapidly affected all kinds of

---

[2]Chinese Website of *Baozou* comic: http://baozoumanhua.com.

[3]Chinese Microblogging platform: http://www.weibo.com/.

[4]A online social networking tool by Tencent: http://www.wechat.com/.

[5]Forbidden City's official Taobao store: https://gugong1925.world.taobao.com/.

这是一个
悲伤逆流成河
的
运气不太好的
明朝皇帝故事

This is a sad story
about an unlucky
emperor of the
Ming Dynasty

总有刁民想害朕

"There is always someone evil who tries to kill me"

Fig. 3.5 Example of *Baozou*-style social media post: words from the microblogging article by Forbidden City's official Taobao store (weibo.com/gugongtaobao) and illustration by Xiaojuan Ma (used with permission)

Fig. 3.6 *Left* Stickers in conventional Internet meme style; *right* stickers in *Baozou* style. (illustration by Xiaojuan Ma and used with permission)

online communications, from instant messaging (IM) such as WeChat (Fig. 3.6) and QQ,[6] micro blogs, e-bulletin boards, to forums.

The popularity of *Baozou* comics is a reflection of an emerging fad of emoticon (particularly digital stickers in IM) engineering (No Author 2016) in China. More and more Chinese Internet users are involved in the creation and dissemination of static images as well as animated GIFs of facial expressions, many of which are in the style of *Baozou* comics. There has been some research on the spread of Internet memes globally (Börzsei 2013, Shifman 2013) We use the *Baozou* comics phenomenon in

---

[6]QQ is another instant messaging tool of Tencent: http://im.qq.com/.

China as a lens to explore the potential socioeconomic factors behind the indulgence in emotion expression in the form of a parody, and discuss some insights into emoticon engineering and its social implications in the situated cultural context.

3.2.4.1 Background

This section reviews the history of *Baozou* comics from its Internet meme roots and more specifically rage comics, the use of emoticons, *kaomoji*, and *emoji* in online communication, and the fad of using stickers in Asia.

Internet Meme, Rage Comics, and *Baozou* Comics

An Internet meme is "a form of visual entertainment" (Börzsei 2013), which gains "influence through online transmission" (Davison 2012) and becomes "replicated via evolution, adaptation, or transformation of the original meme vehicle" (Knobel and Lankshear 2005). More specifically, an Internet meme can be a static image, an animated GIF, a video clip, or a remix of different modalities reproduced or repackaged by anyone out of any existing materials available online (Börzsei 2013, Shifman 2013). Therefore, Internet memes are usually lightweight with low visual quality, which to a certain extent makes them easier to access, replicate, adapt, and spread across the Internet. The memes tend to be simple in style, directing readers to emphasize the embedded message rather than the aesthetic value of the graphics (Börzsei 2013). Note that the message expressed in a meme often deviates from the intent of the original source. The message can be explicitly presented as additional text or implicitly conveyed through the graphical content, sometimes with special effects as visual cues. A commonly seen example of Internet memes is lolcats, *i.e.*, humorous photos of one or more cats with superimposed text, from the Caturday tradition of 4Chan.[7] More examples can be found on the Website Know Your Meme (knowyourmeme.com).

Rage comics are a special genre of Internet memes, originating from an amateur-made four-panel Web comic strip about an angry experience published on 4Chan in 2008. The comic strip mainly consists of a stick figure-style character with a crudely drawn face (a.k.a. rage face) to "show universal emotions"—not restricted to anger or rage—"of varying degrees under a wide variety of circumstances" (Morris 2011). A rage face can be a freehand sketch or copy-pasted from some other sources such as photo, video, cartoon, and Japanese *manga* (Douglas 2014). Some of the most popular rage faces include Forever Alone, Trollface, and Rageguy.[8] Creators can compose elaborate comic strips using rage faces to depict some personal story with a humorous punch line.

---

[7] An image-based bulletin board: http://www.4chan.org.
[8] See http://knowyourmeme.com/memes/rage-comics for more examples.

Rage comics were first introduced to China as *bàozǒu mànhuà* (or *Baozou* comics 暴走漫画) in 2008,[9] and have become increasingly popular among Chinese Internet users since then. The term *bàozǒu* means "out of control," which implies the simple and crude style of the visuals on one hand and its use as a venting channel on the other hand. Initially, *Baozou* comics were mostly amateur comic strips submitted to the *Baozoumanhua*.com Website, telling stress buster jokes or real-life stories with which everyone can somehow resonate (Chen 2014). In recent years, another form of *Baozou* comics has emerged and gained popularity even outside the *Baozoumanhua*.com community.

As part of the fad of using stickers in Chinese social media (No Author 2016) still or animated *Baozou* figures are used as emoticons in electronic and Web messages (Fig. 3.6, right). Besides the classic rage faces, *Baozou* comics creators have added to the collection some new facial expressions extracted from online photos and videos of (Internet) celebrities, such as the famous Yao Ming face. By changing text descriptions and/or varying the background, the same face can express different affects. For example, a friend living in Beijing sent co-author Ma a *Baozou*-style WeChat sticker[10] on the coldest day of the winter of 2016 to tease the north–south divide of central heating in China. The top character in Northern China is showing off while the bottom one in Southern China is pretending to be strong, but they actually share the same face. This process can be called emoticon engineering, because users mainly customize existing *Baozou* faces to indicate their feelings.

Emoticons, *Kaomoji*, *Emoji*, and Stickers

In the narrowest sense, "emoticons" refer to typographic smileys.[11] *Kaomoji*[12] are Japanese-style emoticons that make full use of the Japanese character set in addition to the common symbols. In many occasions, the definition of the term emoticon is extended to include other versions of smileys such as drawings and pictographs. In the scope of this chapter, we use "emoticon" as a general term, *i.e.*, a visual representation of a facial expression, especially as a kind of grassroots creation.

In contrast, *emoji* are stylish graphics originally developed by the Japanese communication company NTT DoCoMo for online communication. The contents of *emoji* range from living beings and everyday objects, to signs and symbols, no longer limited to facial expressions. Although the vocabularies are more or less the same, companies tend to have their own design of the graphics. For example, iOS-phone *emoji* have a different look from those on an Android phone.

---

[9]The copyright of rage comics in China is owned by Xi'an MOMO IT Ltd., the owner of the Website *Baozoumanhua*.com.

[10]See http://ww1.sinaimg.cn/bmiddle/6807d621gw1f0dxsyyh9sj20bc0m8ta5.jpg for the image.

[11]See this article for details: http://www.theguardian.com/technology/2015/feb/06/difference-between-emoji-and-emoticons-explained.

[12]See http://kaomoji.ru/en/ for examples.

Another related concept is stickers: illustrations or animations of characters sometimes attached with witty words and phrases that can be sent in instant messaging (IM) applications to express emotions. In other words, stickers are emoticons designed for IM services. The depiction of facial and bodily expressions in stickers is more elaborative, expressive, and comprehensive than the traditional typographic symbols.

As one says traditionally, a picture is worth a thousand words. Users find digital stickers beneficial, especially in East Asian cultures, because sending a sticker is less cumbersome than typing out the entire message in a logographic script like Chinese (Tabuchi 2014, Guilford 2013, Walther and D'Addario 2001). Furthermore, using stickers can increase the sense of intimacy (Wang 2016), (No Author 2016) and convey feelings that may be awkward to say in words (Szablewicz 2014). Therefore, the fad of using stickers quickly spread across Japanese, Korean, and Chinese users of Asia-based IM services such as Line (Tabuchi 2014) and WeChat (No Author 2016) and extended to other platforms such as Facebook Messenger (Guilford 2013).

Most stickers feature a cute style (Guilford 2013, Tabuchi 2014). However, under the influence of *Baozou* comics, stickers in China have established a special kind of "cuteness" that is very different from the Hello Kitty Japanese *kawaii* style, *i.e.*, a vulgar, wacky appearance with anarchic wit to achieve a parody effect (Li 2014, No Author 2016). Consider WeChat as an example. Not only do many third-party sticker packs ready for downloading have some *Baozou* flavor, but users commonly convert *Baozou*-style images and GIF animations from the Web into stickers or simply make their own. One can find the use of *Baozou* emoticons in other online media as well, ranging from forum and blog posts (Fig. 3.5) to Internet novels. Exploring the socioeconomic context of contemporary China can provide some insights into the popularity of *Baozou* emoticons.

3.2.4.2   Socioeconomic Factors in the Rise of *Baozou* Emoticons in China

Baozou comics were first adopted by young Chinese netizens to vent about amusing or frustrating experiences. Later, it was accepted by a more general population as emoticons. The ugly aesthetics of *Baozou* comics reflects the self-perception of ordinary Chinese Internet users and meets their need for expression in a face-keeping culture.

Subculture of Diǎosī

A nation-wide survey by Sohu showed that 64, 81, and 70% of respondents in their 20s, 30s, and 40s, respectively, considered themselves as a *diǎosī* (屌丝)—a nobody (Kan and Tiscione 2013). *Diǎosī* is an epithet that was originally an insult but has now evolved to be a universal self-ascribed identity, meaning someone born in an ordinary family, with a mediocre look, and having a humble job (Szablewicz 2014). Although often used comically as the polar opposite of the upper class *gāofùshuài* (高富帅, literally means a "tall, rich, and handsome" male) and *báifùměi* (白富美, a "fair-skinned, wealthy, and beautiful" female) (Szablewicz 2014), *diǎosī* actually denotes an average person. According to the 2013 survey, 76% of the respondents from Shanghai, China, took on the *diǎosī* label (Kan and Tiscione 2013), many of whom had college educations and a middle-class incomes.

In other words, a *diǎosī* is not a loser in the traditional sense. Rather, it is a self-perception that one's socioeconomic status is far from perfect in "a pretty person's world" (看脸的世界) where "only the rich can live a willful life" (有钱才能任性). On one hand, *diǎosī* usually admits such imperfection through self-belittlement such as *ǎicuǒqióng* (矮矬穷, *i.e.*, short, ugly, and poor) or humorous satire such as "look at how I look rather than my look" (主要看气质, Fig. 3 right) (Szablewicz 2014). On the other hand, they share the disillusionment of low socioeconomic mobility through *ègǎo* (恶搞, *i.e.*, parody, see Fig. 3.5, for an example) (Szablewicz 2014). For example, the *diǎosī* character portrayed in popular Chinese Web series such as "Unexpectedness (万万没想到)" is usually someone with no background, no money, and no future in reality, but who always keeps the daydream of moving up the socioeconomic ladder. As one of the famous lines from Unexpectedness says, "[I] believe that very soon I will get a promotion and raise, be appointed as the manager, become the CEO, marry a *báifùměi*, and reach the peak in life. [I] get a bit excited just thinking about it."

Baozou comics as a unique combination of cuteness and parody (No Author 2016) fit the multifaceted image of *diǎosī*. First, it is vivid, but not very offensive, to depict the self-mockingly vulgar appearance and life of *diǎosī* using crude, cheap-looking *Baozou*-style characters (Fig. 3.7, left). Sometimes the visuals come with captions in both Chinese and Chinglish ("give you some color to see see" in Fig. 3.6, left) as a self-belittler. Second, a *Baozou* comic has a sense of humor in its gene, and thus can be leveraged to convey the playful nature of *diǎosī* especially in the form of *ègǎo* (Fig. 3.7, right).

Subculture of *Tǔcáo*

Diǎosī often like to tease themselves or assorted phenomena of daily life. The use of mockery is called *tǔcáo* (吐槽 in Chinese and *tsukkomi* in Japanese). This term comes from *Manzai*, a type of team comedy in Japan, in which the *tsukkomi* player points out and corrects the errors and misunderstandings of the *boke* player in a direct, sharp manner (Stacker 2006). In recent years, *tsukkomi* has become a common archetype in Japanese light novels and modern *animé*. Through these channels, Chinese netizens were introduced to the act of *tǔcáo* and have adopted it in everyday scenarios.

However, *tǔcáo* is a challenge to traditional face-keeping culture in China. Self-teasing in public may impair one's own image, while mocking others may be considered as offensive and consequently cause an aversion reaction. Using *Baozou* comics for *tǔcáo* can be an effective risk mitigation strategy. For one thing, *Baozou*

Stay hungry, stay foolish
---Steve Jobs

Fig. 3.7 *Left* A sticker that illustrate a *diǎosī's* self-perception as an onlooker (吃瓜群众); *right* examples of *ègǎo* using a Steve Jobs sticker (illustration by Xiaojuan Ma, used with permission)

faces are universal. People are less likely to associate the characters with a specific person. For another, the exaggerated facial expressions in *Baozou* comics are a well-known device to achieve a comedic effect. As a result, people often view *Baozou*-style *tǔcáo* as a mockery of some common experiences or phenomena rather than a targeted insult. For example, there are two stickers from the same WeChat sticker pack specially made to welcome the year of 2016. One is an ordinary New Year wish, "A whole new year, a whole new me." The other is a *tǔcáo* that can be sent when someone posts that wish, which says "In a few days, someone would post self-deception messages such as 'A whole new year, a whole new me' again."

3.2.4.3 Emotions Expressed in *Baozou* Emoticons

Chinese Internet users, especially those identifying themselves as *diǎosī*, often use *Baozou* emoticons in parody (*ègǎo*) and mockery (*tǔcáo*) of different emotions. This section discusses the underlying rationales, which also indicate the possible reasons why "negative" cuteness becomes popular in Chinese culture, based on 400 *Baozou* faces retrieved from *Baozoumanhua*.com and over 300 *Baozou* stickers collected from WeChat messages.

"Out of Control" Emotions

Chinese people have the tradition of educating children in a culturally appropriate way to display and react to emotions (Wang 2001). On one hand, Chinese people value the negative emotions such as surprise, anger, and dissatisfaction that they perceive as signals of violation of social norm or unfulfillment of social obligations (Yik 2010). On the other hand, they are encouraged to regulate the expression of such emotions in terms of duration, intensity, and frequency, so as not to disrupt interpersonal relationship and social harmony (Bond 1993). Contemporary Chinese are less reluctant to speak out, especially online. However, many people feel that venting through emoticons is more socially acceptable in many occasions than directly saying things in words. This feeling arises because emoticons were initially invented to differentiate jokes from serious content online, meaning that the expressions should not be taken too seriously (Randall 2002).

Before the introduction of *Baozou* emoticons, *kaomoji* was a popular means (and still is in many places) to communicate feelings in forums, games, chat rooms, *etc.* It employs a bigger character set than the single-byte typographic emoticons, and can convey richer affects with faces, actions, objects, and special effects (Fig. 3.8, bottom). However, *kaomoji* are considered as *kawaii* icons and thus favored far more by females (Hjorth 2008). In comparison, *Baozou* emoticons are relatively gender-neutral. They can apply similar visual cues to *kaomoji* and use exaggeration more extensively as a rhetorical device (Fig. 3.8, top).

Besides showing facial expressions as ordinary emoticons do, *Baozou* emoticons can indicate a strong surge of emotion by comically visualizing the intended feeling of getting out of control, such as a lightning strike (*rúléihōngdǐng* 如雷轰顶) for surprise and throwing a table (*xiānzhuō* 掀桌) for anger. Although 14 of the 19 emotion categories in *Baozoumanhua*.com are negative, the same technique can be used to signify positive affect. For example, Fig. 3.9 shows various "thank you, boss" stickers to be used in WeChat messages when participating in digital red packet activities during the Lunar New Year.[13] Characters in the stickers bow, kneel, or kowtow to the sender of the red packet—the boss—for even just a few cents, which hilariously demonstrates appreciation under the *diǎosī* mentality. Such behaviors, however, would be perceived as a severe loss of face in real life.

Subtle or Complicated Emotions

Although the Chinese language has already had a rich vocabulary of emotional terms (Yik 2010), netizens keep inventing new idiom-like Internet slangs to express more subtle or complicated emotions, such as *rénjiānbùchāi* (人艰不拆, "Some lies are better not exposed, as life is already so hard").[14] While existing textual emoticons and *emoji* aim to show common feelings, *Baozou* characters tend to have more emotional depth. Many *Baozou* faces consist of salient features from different basic emotions (Ma, Forlizzi, and Dow 2012), *e.g.*, the character in Fig. 3.10, left. Some faces even deliberately introduce ambiguities. For instance, it is difficult to tell if the character is smiling or crying with one hand over the face if the tears are not drawn (Fig. 3.10, right). Because such designs can lead to different

---

[13]South China Morning Post article on WeChat red packet: http://www.scmp.com/tech/apps-gaming/article/1905882/get-lucky-spring-festival-wechat-adds-sexy-twist-red-envelope.

[14]NYTimes article: http://sinosphere.blogs.nytimes.com/2013/10/27/better-than-a-tweet-using-four-characters-young-chinese-create-internet-idioms-with-a-new-world-of-meaning/?_r=0.

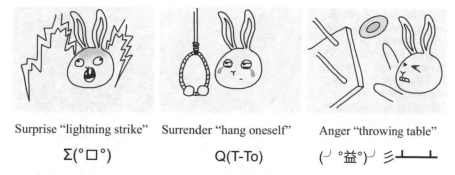

Surprise "lightning strike"   Surrender "hang oneself"   Anger "throwing table"

Σ(°□°)   Q(T-To)   (ノ °益°)ノ ≶⌐━┻

Fig. 3.8 *Top Baozou*-style sticker (illustration by Xiaojuan Ma, used with permission); *bottom* corresponding kaomoji

Fig. 3.9 Various user-made stickers with the message "Thank you, boss" after receiving a WeChat *red* packet (illustration by Xiaojuan Ma, used with permission)

Fearful
Widely opened
eyes and enlarged
pupils
Sad
Tears
Surprised
Widely opened
mouth

"I took an arrow in the knee"
"You are too weak"
"Give me a break"
"Never mind the details"
"It sounds so reasonable that I am speechless"
"It's so beautiful that I dare not look at it"
"Let me cry for a second"
"As long as you are happy about it"

Fig. 3.10 *Left* The Curly Pete face consists of salient facial features of three basic emotions; *right* an examples of one sticker with different messages (illustration by Xiaojuan Ma, used with permission)

Fig. 3.11 An example of textual "overlapping sound (OS)" about the The Emperor's New Clothes. Text under the image: the crowds think that their king is very cute (speechless) today (illustration by Xiaojuan Ma, used with permission)

臣民们觉得国王今天真
是萌(he)萌(he)哒(da)

interpretations of the encoded emotions, they leave room for users to customize the message by attaching different witty phrases and/or adding visual cues (Fig. 3.10, right).

Internal "Overlapping Sound"

Sometimes people do not mean what they say. Chinese Internet users have been using a technique called "overlapping sound (OS)" to illustrate *tǔcáo* as an internal mental activity. OS appears in text such as posts, Internet novels, and news, with the words to be said written in Chinese and the real message written in Pinyin. In the example of 萌(he)萌(he)哒(da) in Fig. 3.11, the post says that the crowd "think that their king is very cute", but it actually means people are speechless. Ambiguous facial expressions in *Baozou* emoticons can serve as good indicators of OS.

3.2.4.4 DIY Emoticon Engineering

In addition to being expressive and evoking, the ability to turn users from pure consumers to producers is another reason why *Baozou* emoticons can quickly gain wide adoption. Depicting facial expressions is usually the most critical and the most difficult part of emoticon design. *Baozou* emoticons make it easier by allowing amateurs to exploit premade faces of *biǎoqíngdì* (表情帝, an individual with rich expressions) from online comics, photos, and videos. Some of the popular examples

Fig. 3.12 *Left* Example of simple customization of a pumpkin head sticker to fit the Lunar New Year theme; *right* examples of how adding simple graphical elements can help disambiguate the emotion, while combining multiple elements can express complicated feelings (illustration by Xiaojuan Ma, used with permission)

include the well-known Yao Ming Face and Jackie Chan's Duang.[15] Some celebrities even published their own *Baozou*-style sticker pack in WeChat sticker store.

To make a *Baozou* emoticon, creators can simply crop out the character from a Web image or a screenshot, turn a photo into a line drawing, or convert a selected video segment to an animated GIF file. Alternatively, people can copy and paste the face onto different cartoon figures, and add other graphical elements such as sweat, flush, shadow, symbols, motion lines, props, and text to further customize the emoticon (Fig. 3.12). This emoticon engineering process can be carried out with ordinary image-editing tools such as Microsoft Paint and Photoshop, or a dedicated *Baozou* comic generator (a.k.a. ragemaker).

3.2.4.5 Discussion

Baozou comic strips encourage readers to put themselves in the character's shoes and reflect upon their own experiences. *Baozou* emoticons instead allow both senders and receivers to separate their image in real life from the representations. For example, in the right sticker of Fig. 3.9, the cat scratches its cheek on the "boss's" arm. The receiver recognizes and accepts the sticker as an expression of appreciation, but will not expect the sender to perform the illustrated action in reality. Such mutual understanding gives *Baozou* sticker users more freedom of choice. Co-author Ma's senior male colleagues actually sent *Baozou* stickers of cute girls and babies.

The fad of stickers has penetrated different age groups. In a Taiwanese talk show called University (大学生了没), the college students shared stories of their parents who are in their 50s and 60s flooding the IM services with stickers. There are similar blog posts on Chinese social media. While the parents seem to master the motivational poster-type of stickers fairly well, Chinese young netizens have discovered a new type of generation gap called "your mom doesn't understand your *Baozou* sticker."

---

[15]BBC article about "Duang": http://www.bbc.com/news/blogs-trending-31689148.

There are several reasons for this gap, which also reveals potential issues in emoticon engineering. First, older Internet users are not very familiar with newly invented Internet slang expressions, and thus they often intuitively take the witty phrases accompanying the emoticons in their literal meaning. For example, a common caption for the "hand-over-face" emoticon (Fig. 3.10, right) is *wǒyěshìzuìle* (我也是醉了, I am drunk). It actually means a person is speechless or knocked out by something shocking, and can be mistaken as a complaint of overdrinking. Misunderstanding frequently occurs when a sticker receiver does not realize that the message uses metaphor or hyperbole. Second, the emphasis of a *Baozou* emoticon is the face, but people may get distracted by other things in the scene. For example, a mother replied, "Don't smoke" to the sad *Baozou* sticker (a crying man taking a cigarette) sent by her son. Third, as mentioned earlier, many *Baozou* expressions are subtle and complicated. Without sufficient visual cues and/or knowledge about the original source of the face, readers may find the emotion difficult to interpret. Fourth, readers may not notice that the emoticon is showing an affect that is different from what is being said; that is, the visual image is serving as the overlapping sound of the words. In the end, the usual response of the younger generation to such miscommunication is, "Never mind. It is just an emotional expression."

In summary, the *Baozou* emoticon phenomenon in China exemplifies an ongoing grassroots creation movement. Its emergence satisfies the need of expression of a new generation of Chinese Internet users. Its ugly aesthetics reflects the self-perception of the users, and is a unique component of the trend of cuteness in many East Asia countries. Easy production, replication, and customization further boost the popularity of *Baozou* emoticons. For similar reasons, the cuteness industry has witnessed a quick rise in China in the past few years. In the next section, we discuss the rise and development of the cuteness industry in China through several examples.

3.3   Cuteness Industry in China

In China, cuteness designs have become pervasive and prominent. The cuteness industry has completely changed how information is communicated, especially in scenarios that used to be considered serious but boring. For example, most of the airlines have recreated their safety videos into cuter, lively animations. Air China, for instance, uses a cartoon panda as the main character for its safety video.[16] In the Beijing International airport, cute signs are set up to explain tax refund policies to oversea travelers (Fig. 3.13). This approach makes information that conventionally seems to be complex and tedious more perceptually fluent to people who may be under stress, fatigue, or cognitive overload.

---

[16]Air China safety video: https://www.youtube.com/watch?v=eBnfWRaCLJ8.

Fig. 3.13 Cute sign about tax refund policies in the Beijing International Airport (photo by Xiaojuan Ma, used with permission)

Fig. 3.14 Example of *Baozou*-style cute souvenir with the Doge image (photo by Quan Li, and used with permission)

Many cute designs have been made into daily necessities in various forms, from stationery, bedding, and accessories, to appliances. The styles of designs found in the market reflect the current taste and trend. For example, Fig. 3.14 shows a pillow

Fig. 3.15 Cute souvenirs designed by the gift shop of the Palace Museum of the Forbidden City (photo by Xiaojuan Ma, used with permission)

printed with the Doge[17] image, a popular Internet meme that is widely used as *Baozou* emoticons in China. It suggests the craze of *Baozou* comics in China these days.

There are several industries in which cuteness designs are applied more systematically. In the following subsections, we choose two industries to demonstrate the impact of cuteness design.

3.3.1 Conventional Culture Industry

The long history of China leaves us with abundant treasures. However, the concept of history may make people feel distant, old, and cold. Merchandise that features ancient Chinese history may give consumers the impression that the products are expensive, fragile, and out of fashion. Consider the Palace Museum of the Forbidden City as an example. The designs printed on the souvenirs sold by the museum used to be mainly replicas of the patterns from antiques in the Forbidden City. In 2014, the cultural creativity design team of the Palace Museum started to add cute elements into their products (Fig. 3.15) and conduct *Baozou*-style soft marketing, a way of playing cute, over the Internet (Fig. 3.5). It is reported that the revenue of the Palace Museum gift shop[18] brought in by these culturally creative products reached 1 billion Chinese Yuan in 2016. In other words, cuteness design has made Chinese cultures and traditions more accessible to younger generations.

---

[17]https://en.wikipedia.org/wiki/Doge_(meme).

[18]One major online store of the Palace Museum: https://palacemuseum.m.tmall.com/.

3.3.2 Internet Technology Industry

The Internet technology (IT) industry is another place where cuteness design plays an important role, particularly in branding and marketing. Most of the major Chinese IT companies, including BAT (*i.e.*, Baidu, Alibaba and Tencent), have franchised their own mascot Intellectual Properties (IPs). They not only place the mascot images in their products and services, but also manufacture assorted souvenirs of the mascots as a channel to communicate their corporate values and beliefs to the employees and customers. Some of the designs incorporate elements from Chinese culture, such as Peking Opera and Spring Festival couplets, increasing the sense of uniqueness and belonging.

In the next subsection, we select a particular case to present a feasible path for stand-alone cuteness business to grow in China, with the possibility of bridging cultural creativity and emerging technologies.

3.3.3 From Original ACG IP to User-Centric IT: A Case Study of How Cuteness Bridges Culture and Technology in China

In this section, we use the A.U franchise created by the Hangzhou A.U Cultural Creativity Co., Ltd. (杭州阿优文化创意有限公司)[19] as an example to study the successful development and possible future direction of the cuteness industry in China.

3.3.3.1 Franchise Positioning and Branding

Hangzhou A.U Cultural Creativity Co., Ltd., was founded in 2009. It is an animation company headquartered in Hangzhou, Zhejiang, China and has successfully built the A.U franchise (Fig. 3.16), an original Chinese ACG IP, since 2012. The A.U franchise targets users aged 5 to 15, about 150 million people in China, and aims to build an ACG-based interactive platform for children and teenagers. The company positions itself as a research-enhanced business in the cultural and creative industry that integrates works and merchandise. It has invested over 150 million Chinese Yuan into building an ecosystem consisting of a renowned children's brand and associated derivatives. For its core ACG business, the company has proposed to create 100 theme games, 1000 episodes of animation, and 10,000 pages of comics of high quality for its target users. As for derivatives of the ACG IP, it has also opened the A.U Academy, an A.U kids clothing brand (Fig. 3.17), A.U

---

[19]http://www.66uu.cn/index_eng.php#en_container.

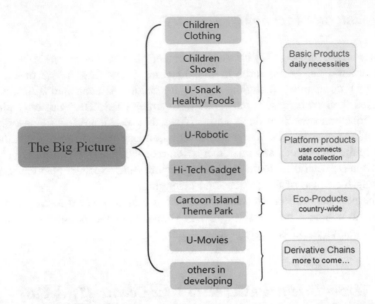

Fig. 3.16 A general diagram of the A.U franchise (copyright © A.U and used with permission)

Fig. 3.17 A.U Children Fashion. (Copyright © A.U, used with permission)

snacks and daily accessories (Fig. 3.18), and a theme park called A.U International Cartoon Island (Fig. 3.19), construction of the theme park started in mid-2015.

According to a nationwide survey conducted by the State Administration of Radio, Film, and Television among primary and secondary school students, 63.3% of the respondents have heard of A.U. As suggested by survey data, about 200 million people have watched various A.U programs. In addition, A.U has received several national and provincial awards, including the "National No. 1 Children Classic Award," the Golden Monkey Award in the Chinese International Animation Festival, and the "Zhejiang Province 5-Star Projects Award." For national branding,

Fig. 3.18 A.U snacks (*left*) and daily accessories (*right*) (copyright © A.U, used with permission)

Fig. 3.19 A.U theme park (copyright © A.U, used with permission)

the company invited the State First-Class director Mr. CAO Xiaohui to direct the A. U cartoon series. For international branding, the company has invited world famous designers, including the former design director of E-Land Kids and Disney Mickey Mouse Kids, for its children fashion brands.

Currently, the A.U company is extending its business to intelligent technologies for children, such as robots and augmented reality (AR) for educational and/or social purposes. It has established the objective of leveraging ACG IP to drive users in order to "make technologies more acknowledgeable of children" (Fig. 3.20). Overall, A.U provides a good example of how the cuteness industry can thrive in contemporary China by (1) identifying a clear target audience; and (2) taking a path

Fig. 3.20 Slogan of A.U: "Having ACG IP drive users; making technologies that acknowledge children more" (copyright © A.U, used with permission)

Fig. 3.21 Example image from the A.U comic (copyright © A.U, used with permission)

of first building a strong IP and brand in the conventional ACG industry and then branching out to closely related cultural, creative, and technological business around its IP (Fig. 3.16).

3.3.3.2   IP Development in Comics and Animation

The A.U IP is established on top of the success of its comics and animation programs. By the end of 2016, A.U Comics (Fig. 3.21) had reached over 8000 pages, equal to about 80 books. The A.U comics series is both published on its site and serialized in journals and magazines, selling more than 7 million issues per month.

The A.U cartoon series (Fig. 3.22) and movie (Fig. 3.23) are also a success. The series has eight seasons with over 300 episodes (6.5 min/episode) in late 2016, and

Fig. 3.22 Examples of posters of A.U animations (copyright © A.U, used with permission)

Fig. 3.23 Flyer for the A.U animated movie (copyright © A.U, used with permission)

is planning to reach its goal of 1000 episodes in six years. Selected as one of the "Top Ten Excellent Chinese Animations" by The State Administration of Radio Film and Television of China, the A.U animations have been broadcasted by about 200 television channels. The cartoon series ranked No. 1 in the ratings of several provincial satellite TV channels in China. The airtime is proximately 470,000 min, potentially bringing in 0.8 billion Chinese Yuan of TV advertisement profit per year. A.U animations have also received over 3 billion hits on major video-streaming networks in China, and host special channels in several video-sharing sites such as tudou.com, potentially contributing 1 billion Chinese Yuan of Internet advertisement profit per year. On the mobile side, the A.U animations are among the top five most popular programs on animation-oriented mobile platform operated by China Mobile. In addition, over 70 A.U mobile theme games are downloadable in Apple and Android app stores.

The A.U IP consists of many characters, among which, the three rabbits and their carrot are particularly used in the company's technological products. As shown in Fig. 3.24, designers deliberately assigned different personalities to the three rabbits. Unlike the conventional naïve and/or innocent type of cuteness, the cuteness of A.

Fig. 3.24 Design of the three main rabbit characters of A.U, *top* to *bottom* on the *left* Tiào Tiào who is always anxious and dressed like a flight pilot; Tù Fēi who is always playing cool and dressed in a purple decorated jacket; and Shuái Ěr who is always slow in reaction and dressed in simple coat (copyright © A.U, used with permission)

Fig. 3.25 Mapping from ACG IP to merchandise design (copyright © A.U, used with permission)

Fig. 3.26 Industrial design of the U Robot (*left*) and user manual (*right*) (copyright © A.U, used with permission)

U's rabbit characters has more depth (see detailed classification in the cuteness taxonomy, Chap. 4) and feels closer and more interesting to the audience. Their approach makes high-tech products using the character designs more attractive to children, the company's target users (Fig. 3.25).

3.3.3.3 From IP to IT: Design and Manufacture

Figures 3.26 and 3.27 demonstrates how A.U's original IP design in ACG became transferred to the industrial design of its technological products, such as (from left to right) portable battery chargers, Tù Fēi smart story machine, Magic Carrot, A.U

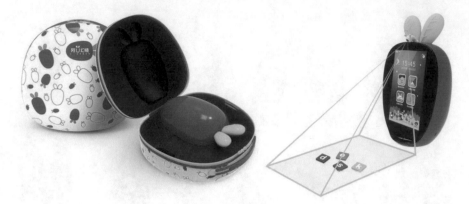

Fig. 3.27 Product and packaging design of the carrot-shaped AR mirror (copyright © A.U, used with permission)

Magic Mirror, and an A.U intelligent robot. Especially for robots (Fig. 3.26) and augmented reality (Fig. 3.27) that are new and perhaps more complicated for children, the intended users, the A.U company's strategy of directly applying the familiar images from its animation makes it much easier to introduce these products into fans' families and classrooms (Fig. 3.25).

3.3.3.4 Marketing and Sales

The A.U company has been collaborating with major Chinese retailers of intelligent products such as PCMall of Sanpower Group (宏图三胞) and Highly Information of TCL (翰林汇), setting up booths or stands for its products to boost sales (Fig. 3.28, left). Globally, A.U products will enter over 300 chain stores of Brookstone in the US and over 90 stores of HAMLEYS in the UK in the near future. Furthermore, for soft marketing purposes, the company has set up many A.U Intelligence Experience centers (Fig. 3.28, right) and A.U Parent-Child Interaction Zones in places where children are likely to gather, such as popular tourist spots, big shopping malls, community centers, and children's fashion chain stores.

In addition, to promote its robot and AR technologies, A.U is actively working with teachers and educators of primary schools (Fig. 3.29). For example, the different parties working together have designed dedicated teaching materials and a maker curriculum that go with the A.U Magic Mirror, and have experimented with intelligent interactive classrooms.

The story of A.U demonstrates that the cuteness industry in China is becoming more mature. The Chinese market and users start to welcome and value local original ACG IPs and their derivatives. Many investors have shown their interests in such cultural and creative industries, which is supported by the Chinese government at different levels.

Fig. 3.28 Marketing strategies of A.U franchise: stand or booth at famous toy stores (*left*) and interactive experience center (*right*) (copyright © A.U, used with permission)

Fig. 3.29 Collaboration with schools and training centers in terms of curriculum design and interactive classroom (copyright © A.U, used with permission)

3.4 Summary

Cuteness has become a widely accepted phenomenon in China. It serves as a universal language that bridges people from different demographic and cultural backgrounds (Fig. 3.30), and plays an increasingly important role in closing the gap between technologies, designs, and users. Although initially influenced by the Japanese, Korean, and Western pop cultures, the conceptualization and representation of cuteness in China have adapted to the unique values/traditions and the economic–social status of the Chinese society.

Fig. 3.30 Cuteness as a universal language (photo by Xiaojuan Ma and used with permission)

References

Bond MH (1993) Emotions and their expression in Chinese culture. J Nonverbal Behav 17 (4):245–262

Börzsei LK (2013) Makes a meme instead: a concise history of internet memes. New Media Stud Mag 7:152–189

Chen SW (2014) *Baozou* manhua (rage comics), internet humour and everyday life. I Continuum 28(5):690–708

Davison P (2012) The language of internet memes. Soc Media Reader 120–134

Douglas N (2014) It's supposed to look like shit: the internet ugly aesthetic. J Vis Cult 13(3):314–339

Guilford G (2013) This company is betting millions that you'll use cartoon bears instead of English. Quartz. http://qz.com/156030/line-is-betting-millions-that-virtual-bears-and-bunnies-will-sweep-the-west/. December 18, 2013 (last checked on May 25, 2017)

Hjorth L (2008) Mobile media in the Asia-Pacific: gender and the art of being mobile. Routledge, UK

Hu HC (1944) The Chinese concepts of "face". Am Anthropol 46(1):45–64

Kan K, Tiscione J (2013) 'Diaosi': understanding China's Generation X. That's Beijing. http://online.thatsmags.com/post/diaosi-understanding-chinas-generation-x

Knobel M, Lankshear C (2005) Memes and affinities: cultural replication and literacy education. In: Annual meeting of the national reading conference, vol 30

Li J (2014) The sticker wars: WeChat's creatives go up against line. http://www.88-bar.com/2014/02/the-sticker-wars-wechats-creatives-go-up-against-line/

Ma X, Forlizzi J, Dow S (2012) Guidelines for depicting emotions in storyboard scenarios. In: 8th International design and emotion conference

Morris K (2011) Making rage comics? Just fine with this English teacher. The daily dot. http://www.dailydot.com/culture/rage-comics-teach-english/

No Author (2015a) China Central Television News (CCTV): Nanjing police teach anti-fraud methods using "Ye Liangchen *Baozou* Comics" (in Chinese). http://news.cntv.cn/2015/10/02/ARTI1443771338069299.shtml

No Author (2015b) Enough, Leave me Alone (in Chinese). Forbidden City's Taobao Store: http://
www.weibo.com/p/1001593903583732031574?from=page_100606_profile&wvr=6&mod=
wenzhangmod

No Author (2016) Face-loving Chinese find new facial expression fad. Xinhua News: http://news.
xinhuanet.com/english/2016-01/28/c_135054074.htm

Randall N (2002) Lingo online: a report on the language of the keyboard generation. MSN
Canada. http://www.arts.uwaterloo.ca/ ∼ nrandall/LingoOnline-finalreport.pdf

Schiphorst RF (2013) The author and the digital craftsman. The author and the digital craftsman.
Faculty of Humanities Master thesis. Utrecht University Repository, https://dspace.library.uu.
nl/handle/1874/273353

Shifman L (2013) Memes in a digital world: reconciling with a conceptual troublemaker. J Comput
Med Commun 18(3):362–377 (2013)

Stacker JF (2006) Manzai: team comedy in Japan's entertainment industry. Understanding humor
in Japan, p 51

Szablewicz M (2014) The 'losers' of China's Internet: Memes as 'structures of feeling' for
disillusioned young netizens. China Inf 28(2):259–275

Tabuchi H (2014) No time to text? Say it with stickers. New York Times. http://www.nytimes.
com/2014/05/26/technology/no-time-to-text-apps-turn-to-stickers.html

Walther JB, D'Addario KP (2001) The impacts of emoticons on message interpretation in
computer-mediated communication. Soc Sci Comput Rev 19(3):324–347

Wang Q (2001) Did you have fun? American and Chinese mother–child conversations about
shared emotional experiences. Cogn Dev 16(2):693–715

Wang SS (2016) More than words? The effect of line character sticker use on intimacy in the
mobile communication environment. Soc Sci Comput Rev 34(4):456–478

Yik M (2010) How unique is Chinese emotion. The Oxford handbook of Chinese psychology,
pp 205–220

Chapter 4
Taxonomy of Cuteness

Cuteness relates to many of the product–service development topics mentioned in other chapters. We proposed a simplified definition of cuteness: a characteristic of a product, person, thing, or context that makes it appealing, charming, funny, desirable, often endearing, memorable, and/or (usually) non-threatening. As one can note from the other chapters, cuteness as a concept is nuanced and complex. From this definition, and looking over published analyses and the images that we have assembled during the past decade, we, the authors, present a taxonomy below to which researchers, designers, software and hardware developers, business managers, and managers may refer. This compilation may be helpful in uncovering new issues or resolving challenges on others.

4.1 Styles of Cuteness

In contemporary culture, people are captivated by an increasingly larger variety of cuteness designs. They find cuteness not only in visual effects (sensory experiences) but also in intangible characteristics such as personality. Sometimes, the combination or contrast of these two aspects will evoke the heart-melting or bonding moments. Of course, people may have different perceptions of cuteness. A design adored by one individual might seem distasteful to others who cannot feel or grasp the "cute attributes (萌点)." People might also change their view of cuteness over time, learning to appreciate the impalpable charm of some designs that are deemed to be ugly at first sight.

An example is LèLè, the mascot of the Nanjing 2014 Youth Olympics Games. Severe criticism arose among the general public when LèLè was first announced. Later, as photos of the mascot falling down on and behind the stage of the youth

© Springer International Publishing AG 2017
A. Marcus et al., *Cuteness Engineering*, Springer Series on Cultural Computing,
DOI 10.1007/978-3-319-61961-3_4

Fig. 4.1 Comparison of conventional "cute" (*left*) and "ugly but cute" (*right*) of a chestnut character (Illustration by Xiaojuan Ma, used with permission)

Olympic games became viral on Weibo, a popular Chinese social media microblogging site, many people started to find LèLè a lovable character, but not in the aesthetic sense.[1] Figure 4.1 illustrates another example of this kind.

No longer homogeneous in representations, cute designs still share some common characteristics. The long interview titled "LIVES: The cat that Rots the Intellect" with cartoonist Jim Davis, the father of Garfield, a fat lazy grumpy feline character, by Walter Shapiro from Washington Post back in 1982, provides some valuable insights.[2] Although one of Garfield's favorite sayings is "Cute rots the intellect," Davis does not consider his creation a "pretty sight," at least not in the conventional sense, "None of that is cute. Look at that look in his eye. There's something else on his mind. He's looking ornery." But why can Garfield hold its own corner in a "Hallmark gift store that sells all these—the tabernacle of American cute" as Walter pointed out? One of the key design implications reflected in Davis's responses is that the character should be maximally inoffensive, which consists of several aspects.[3]

- *No referencing to sensitive issues*
  As Davis stressed in the interview, "It's a conscious effort to include everyone as readers … In an effort to keep the gags broad, the humor general and applicable to everyone, I deal mainly with eating and sleeping. That applies to everyone, anywhere." In other words, a cute design should be inclusive and not threatening. It should provide physical or behavior cues that users can somewhat relate to, so as not to trigger any defense mechanism from an evolutionary perspective, as cuteness in some sense is a perception of vulnerability (Hildebrandt and Fitzgerald 1979; Lorenz 1971). This may explain why baby-like figures, animals, and abstract characters are popular choices of cute designs, because "people aren't threatened by (them) … (and they aren't) going to step on anyone's feet."

---

[1]https://www.zhihu.com/question/24484040.

[2]https://www.washingtonpost.com/archive/opinions/1982/12/12/lives-the-cat-that-rots-the-intellect/d6ed28c6-bee3-41ad-81f2-1839b34b87b1/?utm_term=.71a9d097874c.

[3]http://www.huffingtonpost.com/entry/garfield-facts-jim-davis_us_55b64d2fe4b0a13f9d191201.

- *Perceptually simple*

  Davis emphasizes on the fact that "the Garfield art is very, very simple," so that "nothing distracts the eye … (and) they see the characters, the expression."
- *With high predictability of personality*

  Davis highlighted the benefit of having inner traits to character establishment in the interview, "personality in the long run was going to be the real payoff … I felt a selfish, cynical, lazy type of character with a little soft underbelly would endure." More specifically, he postulated that it is the predictability of the personality in the long run that helps maintain the character and its story. Humans in general fear unknown and change. If users can see what is coming and where it is coming from in a design, they may be more relaxing in their experience with the design.

  However, predictability does not necessarily mean that the personality is shallow. Actually, Garfield makes comments that many adults would find inspiring, which comes from his dynamic, deep personality. Also, a predictable personality can have multiple facets, just that each facet is somewhat transparent to viewers. For example, Garfield is mean to almost every living being but loves his teddy bear. This little twist in his personality is as "close as he gets to cute."

Overall, the style of cuteness can come from sensory experience or character traits. The two can agree or contradict with each other. Hence, in this chapter, we construct the taxonomy of cuteness in the list below based on these two aspects as well as their inter-relationships:

I. Cuteness by Attribute

    A. Sensory Cute

        a. Gender-specific Cute

            i. Sexy Cute
           ii. Lolita Cute (萝莉萌)
         iii. Uniform Cute (制服萌)

        b. Gender-neutral Cute

            i. Baby Cute
           ii. Animal Cute

    B. Personality Cute

        a. Positive Cute

            i. Naïve Cute (天然萌)
           ii. Soft Cute (软萌)

    b. Negative Cute

        i. Ugly Cute (丑萌)
       ii. Stupid Cute (蠢萌)
      iii. Slow-witted Cute (呆萌)
      iv. Awkward Cute (囧萌)
       v. Lurid, Vulgar, or Anarchic Cute (贱萌)

II. Cuteness by Contrast (反差萌)

  A. One-dimensional

    a. Cute by Tangible Contrast

        i. Appearance
       ii. Strength
      iii. Instrument
      iv. Transformation

    b. Cute by Intangible Contrast

        i. Personality change

  B. Multidimensional

    a. Cute by Appearance–Personality Contrast

        i. Scheming (腹黑)
       ii. Smolderingly Passionate (闷骚)

    b. Cute by Behavior–Personality Contrast

        i. Stubbornly Softhearted (Tsundere, ツンデレ, 傲娇)

    c. Cute by Identity–Personality/Behavior Contrast

        i. Social Status
       ii. Name
      iii. Fame

    d. Cute by Appearance–Identity Contrast

        i. Age
       ii. Gender (伪娘, 伪郎)
      iii. Profession

(*Note*: In this taxonomical organization of cuteness based on sensory experiences or character traits, Chinese translations are given to help those with a knowledge of Chinese to understand the nuances of the terminology better).

    In much of the rest of this chapter, we use instances extracted from an unusually useful and extensive collection of manga imagery, the Manga109 dataset[4] (Matsui

---

[4]http://www.manga109.org/index_en.php.

et al. 2015), and other real-world examples to define each style of cuteness and illustrate the lowest common denominator of the corresponding (visual) design.

I. Cuteness by Attribute

We refer to cuteness by attribute as the styles of design that associate the sense of likeableness with either the appearance or inner traits depicted through language, facial expressions and behaviors that can be perceived by viewers.

I.A. Sensory Cute

Sensory cute is evoked purely by sensory experiences, such as visual appearance and sound. It is the most explicit type of cuteness, and can usually be felt or recognized at first sight.

I.A.a. Gender-specific Cute

When we say someone is cute in everyday conversations, the features to which we are referring might be different according to the gender of the target. Similarly in design, certain cuteness styles are associated with a particular gender group, female in most of the cases. We may further divide female-specific cuteness into two classes that attract people's eyes for different reasons.

I.A.a.i. Sexy Cute

The first class is sexy cute in a conventional sense. A representative figure in reality is the iconic movie star Marilyn Monroe, for example, in many scenes of the movie "Some Like it Hot."

Sexy cuteness is commonly conveyed by a nicely proportioned "8" shaped body, sultry body posture and language, and slinky garments that can reveal body curves such as a full bust and hips and long thin legs. Figure 4.2 presents sexy cute girls in ordinary clothing (with special cuts) or swimsuits, and Fig. 4.3 shows flirtatious characters in special costumes.

I.A.a.ii. Loli Cute (萝莉萌)

In contrast, loli cute (the word loli comes from the 1962 movie "Lolita") is used, for manga in particular, for young (school) girls, featuring liveliness rather than seductiveness. Characters in this category usually do not have a curvy body shape. Instead, they tend to wear school uniforms as well as doll-like accessories such as hair band and animal ears (*e.g.*, cat and bunny ears). See Fig. 4.4 for examples.

I.A.a.iii. Uniform Cute (制服萌)

A third category of cuteness is associated with the uniform of certain professions, *e.g.*, maid, nurse, and waitress. Different from the garments for sexy cuteness, the common clothing features shared among the cute characters in this category include long skirt, lace, apron, and sometimes hat or hair band (Fig. 4.5).

ラブひな LoveHina
Copyright © Akamatsu Ken

あっけら貫刃帖 AkkeraKanjinchou
Copyright © Kobayashi Yuki

1・2・3でキメてあげる
Count3DeKimeteAgeru
Copyright © Omiya Naoi

サラダデイズ SaladDays
Copyright © Inokuma Shinobu

爆烈！ かんふー娘 BakuretsuKungFugirl
Copyright © Ueda Miki

Fig. 4.2 Examples of sexy cute: ordinary clothing with sexy poses (*left two*) and special clothing from daily life (*right three*) (*Image source* Manga109 dataset, used with permission)

BEMADER・P BEMADER_P
Copyright © Hasegawa Yuichi

ドールガン DollGun
Copyright © Deguchi Ryusei

じじばばファイト！ JijiBabaFight
Copyright © Nishikawa Shinji

ねこだま Nekodamaデュアルジャスティス DualJustice
Copyright © Ebihurai Copyright © Takeyama Yusuke

Fig. 4.3 Examples of sexy costumes (*Image source* Manga109 dataset, used with permission)

ありさ2 Arisa
Copyright © Yagami Ken

メテオさんストライクです！
MeteoSanStrikeDesu
Copyright © Takuji

太陽にスマッシュ！
TaiyouNiSmash
Copyright © Ayumi Yui

てんしのはねとアクマのシッポ
TensiNoHaneToAkumaNoShippo
Copyright © Kiriga Yuki

ヒーリング・プラネット HealingPlanet
Copyright © Sakurano Minene

ジョバレ Jovolley
Copyright © Shirai sanjirou

あくはむ Akuhamu
Copyright © Arai Satoshi

サイコスタッフ PsychoStaff
Copyright © Mizukami Satoshi

Fig. 4.4 Examples of Lolita cute (*Image source* Manga109 dataset, used with permission)

黒井戸眼科 KuroidoGanka ゆめ色クッキング YumeiroCooking ラブひな LoveHina ヒーリング・プラネット HealingPlanet
Copyright © Taira Masami   Copyright © Kurita Riku   Copyright © Akamatsu Ken   Copyright © Sakurano Minene

Fig. 4.5 Examples of uniform cute characters (*Image source* Manga109 dataset, used with permission)

I.A.b. **Gender-neutral Cute**

The above-mentioned cuteness styles have clear gender cues, and thus may be more attractive to certain demographic groups. In contrast, gender-neutral cuteness, baby cute, and animal cute in particular, would have a much broader audience and wider applications.

I.A.b.i. **Baby Cute**

By baby cute, we refer to cuteness of human characters, typically during and before the age for kindergarten. At this stage, it is hard to tell their gender by face only. Cute babies have a round face (about 1/3 of the body), fat hands and feet, and big eyes (about 1/2 of the face) (Fig. 4.6).

Artists and designers can follow these characteristics to convert an ordinary (young) adult character to a baby cute version (for examples, see Fig. 4.7).

I.A.b.ii. **Animal Cute**

Animal cuteness, as suggested by the name, consists of cute sensory attributes usually seen on real of fictitious animal figures. As shown in Figs. 4.8 and 4.9, these features include fat, round body (head), disproportionally big/long/fat ears and tails, particularly big or tiny eyes, and special decorative accessories such as ribbons, butterfly bows, tiny wings, hats, and other props.

I.B. **Personality Cute**

Sensory cuteness could be directly perceived and is considered a pleasure for the eyes. The tactics to create sensory cute characters are relatively easy to perform. However, in recent years, we observe an increasing trend in which the cuteness of a figure is conveyed not through its appearance but via its personality traits as

燃える！お兄さん
MoeruOnisan
Copyright © Sato Tadashi

君は僕の太陽だ
KimiHaBokuNoTaiyouDa
Copyright © Toujo Kazumi

魔夜の赤い靴
MayaNoAkaiKutsu
Copyright © Aida Mayumi

幼稚園ぼうえい組
YouchienBoueigumi
Copyright © Tenya

ひなぎく見参！一本桜花町編
HinagikuKenzan
Copyright © Sakurano Minene

ジョバレ
Jovolley
Copyright © Shirai sanjirou

銀のキメイラ
GinNoChimera
Copyright © Nakamura Chisato

Fig. 4.6 Examples of baby cute (*Image source* Manga109 dataset, used with permission)

日常スープ NichijouSoup
Copyright © Shindou Uni

レヴァリアース ReveryEarth
Copyright © Yama Miyuki

Fig. 4.7 Examples of baby-cutified characters (*Image source* Manga109 dataset, used with permission)

みすて？ないでデイジー MisutenaideDaisy
Copyright © Nagano Noriko

あくはむ Akuhamu
Copyright © Arai Satoshi

ねこだま Nekodama
Copyright © Ebihurai

ランスロットフルスロットル
LancelotFullThrottle
Copyright © Dynamic Tarou

てんしのはねとアクマのシッポ
TensiNoHaneToAkumaNoShippo
Copyright © Kiriga Yuki

あくはむ Akuhamu
Copyright © Arai Satoshi

タップ君の探偵室 TapkunNoTanteisitsu
Copyright © Hukuyama Kei

ヒーリング・プラネット HealingPlanet
Copyright © Sakurano Minene

ヒーリング・プラネット HealingPlanet
Copyright © Sakurano Minene

ラブひな LoveHina
Copyright © Akamatsu Ken

ひなぎく見参！一本桜花町編
HinagikuKenzan
Copyright © Sakurano Minene

てんしのはねとアクマのシッポ
TensiNoHaneToAkumaNoShippo
Copyright © Kiriga Yuki

Fig. 4.8 Examples of cute animals; from *top* to *bottom*: (semi-) realistic depiction, cartoony depiction, and animal-like fictitious characters (*Image source* Manga109 dataset, used with permission)

revealed over time. This phenomenon is particularly prevalent among characters with background stories (*e.g.*, a movie, a cartoon series, or a comic strip) that gives more richness and depth to the characters' images. The audiences learn to like the characters as their personalities unfold or develop with the progress of the story. Depending on the polarity of the personality, we can further divide personality cuteness into positive and negative cute.

Fig. 4.9 Examples of cute animals that follow the disproportionate and spherical principles (*Image source* Manga109 dataset, used with permission)

I.B.a. **Positive Cute**

Positive cuteness is associated with meritorious personal qualities in the conventional sense.

I.B.a.i. **Naïve Cute** (天然萌)

A naïve cute character is natural, unaffected, and optimistic. There are several ways to depict naïve cute.

The first method is to draw an emotionless face (Fig. 4.10) to suggest that the character is not judgmental, artificial, or insincere.

The second method is to show curiosity of the characters, especially through stars in their eyes (Fig. 4.11).

The third method is to render a happy, worry/fear-free image of the characters, usually with arms wide open, running around or walking in big steps, jumping in the air, *etc.* (Fig. 4.12).

The fourth method is to illustrate that the characters could be easily satisfied and entertained, through scenes like enjoying tasty food (Fig. 4.13) singing, dancing, and playing with animals (Fig. 4.14). These characters know how to appreciate and enjoy life.

I.B.a.ii. **Soft Cute** (软萌)

Soft cuteness is associated more with characters that are a bit shy, innocent, and sweet, but not intrusive. They often have an innocent look with blush on the face, with gestures such as hands on the chest/on the chin/over the mouth (Fig. 4.15) and/or postures like tilting the head, leaning, or hiding (Fig. 4.16). Although soft cuteness is more commonly seen in female figures, other characters applying these facial expressions, gestures, and body languages could also achieve a similar perception.

I.B.b. **Negative Cute**

There is a large category of cuteness arising from negative personalities that are traditionally disfavored, but then began to be seen and adored by more and more people.

Fig. 4.10 Examples of (emotionless) naïve cute (*Image source* Manga109 dataset, used with permission)

Fig. 4.11 Examples of (curious) naïve cute (*Image source* Manga109 dataset, used with permission)

Fig. 4.12 Examples of (worry-free) naïve cute (*Image source* Manga109 dataset, used with permission)

Fig. 4.13 Examples of worry-free expressions while eating (*Image source* Manga109 dataset, used with permission)

ぶらり鉄扇捕物帳
BurariTessenTorimonocho
Copyright © Sasaki Atsushi

ハムレット
Hamlet
Copyright © Minamoto Tarou

Oh!われら劣等生徒会
OhWareraRettouSeitokai
Copyright © Aida Mayumi

密・リターンズ!
HisokaReturns
Copyright © Yagami Ken

Fig. 4.14 Examples of worry-free expressions while playing (*Image source* Manga109 dataset, used with permission)

ありさ2
Arisa
Copyright © Yagami Ken

爆烈!かんふー娘
BakuretsuKungFugirl
Copyright © Ueda Miki

空っぽハイスクール
KarappoHighschool
Copyright © Takaguchi Satosumi

太陽にスマッシュ!
TaiyouNiSmash
Copyright © Ayumi Yui

魔夜の赤い靴
MayaNoAkaiKutsu
Copyright © Aida Mayumi

さまよえる少年に純愛を
SamayoeruSyonenNiJunaiWo
Copyright © Karikawa Seyu

その気でABC
SonokiDeABC
Copyright © Tashiro Kimu

Fig. 4.15 Examples of soft cute (*Image source* Manga109 dataset, used with permission)

とっておきのABC TolleokINoABC
Copyright © Aida Mayumi

ねこだま Nekodama
Copyright © Ebihurai

ぶらり鉄扇捕物帳 BurariTessenTorlmonocho
Copyright © Sasaki Atsushi

Fig. 4.16 Examples of animals and male character with soft cuteness (*Image source* Manga109 dataset, used with permission)

I.B.b.i. **Ugly, Evil, or Scary Cute** (丑萌)

Characters under this subclass are usually distasteful in appearance. However, there is a sentiment in social media that "when something is unpleasant to a certain extent, it becomes cute" (丑到深处自然萌), which is a kind of opposite of the uncanny variety.

Ugly cute usually comes with big eyes with small pupils that pop up or are widely set apart (Fig. 4.17). Crazy behaviors often accompany the unattractive looks.

Evil cute characters have half-opened sharp eyes, sometimes with a smirk (Fig. 4.18).

がらくた屋まん太　みすて?ないでデイジー　タップ君の探偵室　　OLランチ　魔法使い養成専門マジックスター学院☆☆☆
GarakutayaManta   MisutenaideDaisy   TapkunNoTanteisitsu   OL_Lunch   MagicStarGakuin
Copyright © Nouda Tatsuki Copyright © Nagano Noriko Copyright © Hukuyama Kei Copyright © Sanri Youko Copyright © Minamisawa Hishika

Fig. 4.17 Examples of ugly cute (*Image source* Manga109 dataset, used with permission)

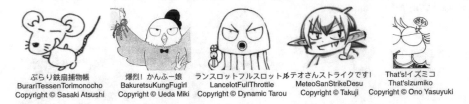

ぶらり鉄扇捕物帳　　爆烈! かんふー娘　ランスロットフルスロット　メテオさんストライクです!　That's!イズミコ
BurariTessenTorimonocho BakuretsuKungFugirl LancelotFullThrottle MeteoSanStrikeDesu That'sIzumiko
Copyright © Sasaki Atsushi Copyright © Ueda Miki Copyright © Dynamic Tarou Copyright © Takuji Copyright © Ono Yasuyuki

Fig. 4.18 Examples of evil cute (*Image source* Manga109 dataset, used with permission)

Scary cute figures have two typical designs: (1) solid, dark, pupil-free eyes, and sharp teeth (Fig. 4.19) and (2) triangular eyes with scar(s) on the face (Fig. 4.20).

I.B.b.ii. **Stupid Cute** (蠢萌)

Stupid cute characters are comical, often making mistakes and messing up the situation. Their most frequently seen features are enlarged eyes with shrunken pupils (Fig. 4.21). Some variables include other features, like exaggerated mouths (Fig. 4.22) and a flood of tears (Fig. 4.23). Figure 4.24 demonstrates that by simply applying dull looking eyes and mouth, one can convert any character into its stupid cute version.

I.B.b.iii. **Slow-witted Cute** (呆萌)

Different from stupid cuteness, slow-witted cuteness refers to the feeling that something is slow in reaction. Characters of this kind may have tiny, dot-like eyes signaling that they are totally confused (Fig. 4.25) or droopy eyes as if they are half-sleep or daydreaming (Fig. 4.26).

てんしのはねとアクマのシッポ　ワレワレハ、オニデアル　メテオさんストライクです!　プレイヤーは眠れない
TensiNoHaneToAkumaNoShippo WarewareHaOniDearu MeteoSanStrikeDesu PrayerHaNemurenai
Copyright © Kiriga Yuki Copyright © Nakayama Noriko Copyright © Takuji Copyright © Kurosawa Tetsuya, Masaki Hidehisa

Fig. 4.19 Examples of scary cute with dark eyes (*Image source* Manga109 dataset, used with permission)

じじばばファイト!
JijiBabaFight
Copyright © Nishikawa Shinji

燃える! お兄さん
MoeruOnisan
Copyright © Sato Tadashi

Fig. 4.20 Examples of scary cute with facial scar (*Image source* Manga109 dataset, used with permission)

がらくた屋まん太
GarakutayaManta
Copyright © Nouda Tatsuki

ワレワレハ、オニデアル
WarewareHaOniDearu
Copyright © Nakayama Noriko

その気でABC
SonokiDeABC
Copyright © Tashiro Kimu

うちの猫ず日記
UchiNoNyan'sDiary
Copyright © Gasan

どんぶらこっこ
Donburakokko
Copyright © Nakanuki Eri

Fig. 4.21 Examples of stupid cute with exaggerated eyes (*Image source* Manga109 dataset, used with permission)

レヴァリアース
ReveryEarth
Copyright © Yama Miyuki

燃える! お兄さん
MoeruOnisan
Copyright © Sato Tadashi

アンバランス・トーキョー
UnbalanceTokyo
Copyright © Uchida Minako

うちの猫ず日記
UchiNoNyan'sDiary
Copyright © Gasan

ワレワレハ、オニデアル
WarewareHaOniDearu
Copyright © Nakayama Noriko

Fig. 4.22 Examples of stupid cute with exaggerated eyes and mouth (*Image source* Manga109 dataset, used with permission)

I.B.b.iv. **Awkward Cute** (囧萌)

Awkward cuteness is often captured when characters encounter some difficult, embarrassing situations. People may find them cute because they are (1) trying very hard to solve the problem with a squeezed face, although the process and results could still be frustrating (Fig. 4.27). (2) shocked to an extent that the facial expressions and movements are all frozen (Fig. 4.28), or (3) suppressing their anger but cannot help revealing their disgust through their squinty eyes as well as twitching eyelids and mouth corners (Fig. 4.29).

燃える！お兄さん
MoeruOnisan
Copyright © Sato Tadashi

１・２・３でキメてあげる
Count3DeKimeteAgeru
Copyright © Omiya Naoi

テオさんストライクです！
MeteoSanStrikeDesu
Copyright © Takuji

Fig. 4.23 Examples of stupid cute with exaggerated eyes and tears (*Image source* Manga109 dataset, used with permission)

Fig. 4.24 Examples of converting characters to stupid cute versions (Illustration by Xiaojuan Ma, used with permission)

ゆめ色クッキング
YumeiroCooking
Copyright © Kurita Riku

ＰＬＡＮＥＴ７
PLANET7
Copyright © Takeya Shuji

学園ノイズ
GakuenNoise
Copyright © Inohara Daisuke

ワレワレハ、オニデアル
WarewareHaOniDearu
Copyright © Nakayama Noriko

日常スープ
ichijjouSoup
Copyright © Shindou Uni

ぶらり鉄扇捕物帳
BurariTessenTorimonocho
Copyright © Sasaki Atsushi

むこうきずのチョンボ
MukoukizuNoChonbo
Copyright © Minamoto Tarou

Fig. 4.25 Examples of slow-witted (in reaction) cute (*Image source* Manga109 dataset, used with permission)

うちの猫'ず日記
UchiNoNyan'sDiary
Copyright © Gasan

爆烈！かんふー娘
BakuretsuKungFugirl
Copyright © Ueda Miki

はるかリフレイン
HarukaRefrain
Copyright © Ito Shinpei

ハムレット
Hamlet
Copyright © Minamoto Tarou

Fig. 4.26 Examples of slow-witted (half-sleep, energy-less) cute (*Image source* Manga109 dataset, used with permission)

やまとの羽根   みすて?ないでデイジータナベキヨミ短編集・桃山灰神楽   やさしい悪魔   ひなぎく見参! 一本桜花町編
YamatoNoHane   MisutenaideDaisy   MomoyamaHaikagura   YasasiiAkuma   HinagikuKenzan
Copyright © Saki Kaori Copyright © Nagano Noriko Copyright © Tanabe Kiyomi Copyright © Hanada Sakumi Copyright © Sakurano Minene

Fig. 4.27 Examples of awkward (frustrated) cute with squeezed eyes (*Image source* Manga109 dataset, used with permission)

青すぎる春   サイコスタッフ   密・リターンズ!   その気でＡＢＣ
AosugiruHaru   PsychoStaff   HisokaReturns   SonokiDeABC
Copyright © Okuda Momoko Copyright © Mizukami Satoshi Copyright © Yagami Ken Copyright © Tashiro Kimu

Fig. 4.28 Example of awkward (shocked) cute with frozen expression and cold sweat (*Image source* Manga109 dataset, used with permission)

ぶらり鉄扇捕物帳   ワレワレハ、オニデアル   どんぶらこっこ
BurariTessenTorimonocho   WarewareHaOniDearu   Donburakokko
Copyright © Sasaki Atsushi   Copyright © Nakayama Noriko   Copyright © Nakanuki Eri

Fig. 4.29 Example of awkward (angry/disgusted) cute with squinted eyes (*Image source* Manga109 dataset, used with permission)

I.B.b.v. **Lurid (Vulgar, Arrogant) Cute** (贱萌)

Lurid cuteness can be divided into finer subclasses according to the actual personalities and emotions expressed.

Vulgar cute characters can be thinking about something sexually romantic, in particular for males, who have a blush on the face and curvy eyes with tiny pupils looking up or to the side (Figs. 4.30 and 4.31), or making fun of someone else through off-color humor (Fig. 4.32).

Arrogant cute characters tend to cheer for their own success, especially over others' failure, in an exaggerated manner, such as chest-puffing, big laughter, victory gestures, *etc.* (Fig. 4.33).

その気でＡＢＣ
SonokiDeABC
Copyright © Tashiro Kimu

がらくた屋まん太
GarakutayaManta
Copyright © Nouda Tatsuki

黄昏通信
TasogareTsushin
Copyright © Tanaka Masato

ボクはしたたか君
BokuHaShitatakaKun
Copyright © Shinzawa Motoei

Fig. 4.30 Examples of vulgar cute (male) characters (*Image source* Manga109 dataset, used with permission)

燃える！お兄さん
MoeruOnisan
Copyright © Sato Tadashi

タップ君の探偵室
TapkunNoTanteisitsu
Copyright © Hukuyama Kei

爆烈！かんふー娘
BakuretsuKungFugirl
Copyright © Ueda Miki

ねこだま
Nekodama
Copyright © Ebihurai

Fig. 4.31 Examples of vulgar cute animal characters (*Image source* Manga109 dataset, used with permission)

GOOD KISS！Ver.2.0 GOOD_KISS_Ver2
Copyright © Kawakata Kaoru

ジョバレ Jovolley
Copyright © Shirai sanjirou

ゆめ色クッキング YumeiroCooking
Copyright © Kurita Riku

Fig. 4.32 Examples of vulgar expressions on other matter (*Image source* Manga109 dataset, used with permission)

うるとら☆イレブン UltraEleven
Copyright © Yabuno Tenya, Watanabe Tatsuya

ワレワレハ、オニデアル WarewareHaOniDearu
Copyright © Nakayama Noriko

最速!! Saisoku
Copyright © Matsuda Naomasa

Fig. 4.33 Examples of arrogant cute (*Image source* Manga109 dataset, used with permission)

むこうきずのチョンボ
MukoukizuNoChonbo
Copyright © Minamoto Tarou

ばいばいC-BOY ByebyeC-BOY
Copyright © Aida Mayumi

君は僕の太陽だ KimiHaBokuNoTaiyouDa
Copyright © Toujo Kazumi

Fig. 4.34 Examples of provocative cute (*Image source* Manga109 dataset, used with permission)

ぶらり鉄扇捕物帳
BurariTessenTorimonocho
Copyright © Sasaki Atsushi

その気でＡＢＣ
SonokiDeABC
Copyright © Tashiro Kimu

Fig. 4.35 Examples of a scene with an angry character, an awkward character, and a naïve character (*Image source* Manga109 dataset, used with permission)

Another type of arrogant characters are those who like to express their provocation and contempt through a smug facial expression and looking from the corner of their eyes (Fig. 4.34).

When characters with different kinds of personality-based cuteness gather in a scene, the humorous effect is further boosted, as shown in Fig. 4.35.

II. Cuteness by Contrast (反差萌)

Unlike sensory and personality cuteness, certain senses of cuteness are created through the contrast of different attributes.

II.A. One-dimensional

Such contrast could come from the same dimension in the design space.

II.A.a. Cute by Tangible Contrast

Some of the contrast could be directly perceived by the senses.

II.A.a.i. Appearance

One of the most frequently seen examples of tangible contrast is related to appearance, usually between the face and clothing/accessories. As shown in Fig. 4.36, the character (in the *middle*) has a scary face and always chews a

幼稚園ぼうえい組
YouchienBoueigumi
Copyright © Tenya

Fig. 4.36 Example of a character with a scary face dressed up in cute costume (*Image source* Manga109 dataset, used with permission)

toothpick and thus is often identified as a tough gangster (left). However, when he dresses up in a bunny costume (right) with the same look on his face, people find him really cute.

II.A.a.ii. **Strength**

A character is considered cute when its physical strength/ability does not match with the impression given by its appearance, such as a child-looking character that can lift weights heavier than what a normal adult can handle (Fig. 4.37) or a muscular fellow who is actually weak.

II.A.a.iii. **Instrument**

Similarly, using tools unfit for the image of a character can also evoke the feeling of cuteness, such as little kids waving a sword taller and bigger than them, or a well-built adult using swimming tube in the pool (Fig. 4.38).

あっけら貫刃帖 AkkeraKanjinchou   無敵冒険シャクマ MutekiBouke
Copyright © Kobayashi Yuki   Copyright © Shakuma   Kazuna Kei

Fig. 4.37 Examples of characters of child-like appearance but superior physical strength (*Image source* Manga109 dataset, used with permission)

Fig. 4.38 Example of a
character with a muscular
body using a swimming tube
(*Image source* Manga109
dataset, used with permission)

燃える! お兄さん MoeruOnisan
Copyright © Sato Tadashi

Fig. 4.39 Examples of
characters transformed in size
(*left*) or appearance (*right*)
(*Image source* Manga109
dataset, used with permission)

ばいばいC-BOY
ByebyeC-BOY
Copyright © Aida Mayumi

日常スープ
NichijouSoup
Copyright © Shindou Uni

II.A.a.iv. Transformation

Sometimes, the tangible contrast occurs in the presence of physical transformation.
For instance, a small fat, lazy cat turns into a big, wild monster (Fig. 4.39, left) or a
serious character turns into a tree trunk (Fig. 4.39, right).

II.A.b. Cute by Intangible Contrast

Cuteness by contrast can also come from intangible features.

II.A.b.i. Personality change

Quick, obvious changes in personality are one of such sources of cuteness. As
exemplified in Fig. 4.40, the character on the left quickly switches from a poker
face to a vulgar expression. The character in the *middle* can freely alter its image
between an angry bird and an innocent, harmless chick. The character on the right is
serious and strict most of the time. Therefore, it is comical when she bursts into big
laughter in front of something funny.

II.B. Multidimensional

Contrast-based cuteness can involve different facets of the design space.

ボクはしたたか君
BokuHaShitatakaKun
Copyright © Shinzawa Motoei

幼稚園ぼうえい組
YouchienBoueigumi
Copyright © Tenya

空っぽハイスクール
KarappoHighschool
Copyright © Takaguchi Satosumi

Fig. 4.40 Examples of characters that switch between different personalities (*Image source* Manga109 dataset, used with permission)

II.B.a. **Cute by Appearance–Personality Contrast**

One of the most typical examples of multidimensional contrast-based cuteness is the result of conflicts between ones' appearance and personality. We present the following two instances to showcase the nuances.

II.B.a.i. **Scheming** (腹黑)

Scheming cuteness occurs on characters that seem to be harmless and innocent but are actually devious. For example, the *middle* character in Fig. 4.41 looks like a girl with a soft temperament, but she is indeed quite tough.

Fig. 4.41 Example of characters with appearance–personality contrast (*Image source* Manga109 dataset, used with permission)

てんしのはねとアクマのシッポ
TensiNoHaneToAkumaNoShippo
Copyright © Kiriga Yuki

II.B.a.ii. **Smolderingly Passionate** (闷骚)

Smolderingly passionate characters often wear a stony face and dull clothes, but inside they are rather playful. The character on the right in Fig. 4.41 is such an example, which wears a suit with bunny ears.

II.B.b. **Cute by Behavior–Personality Contrast**

The differences between how people behave and their inner traits can also evoke the sense of cuteness.

II.B.b.i. **Stubbornly Softhearted (Tsundere, ツンデレ, 傲娇)**

One of the most commonly seen examples in this category is stubbornly softhearted cuteness. Characters with such traits tend to speak and behave viciously, like to say "no," or often play hard to get (Fig. 4.42). However, they actually have a soft heart, always willing to help others or compromise, although they never explicitly reveal it (Fig. 4.41, left).

II.B.c. **Cute by Identity–Personality/Behavior Contrast**

The differences between an image associated with one's identity and the actual behaviors/traits can lead to the perception of cuteness as well.

II.B.c.i. **Social Status**

The identity could be related to social status. The snail in the *middle* of Fig. 4.43 is a devil who wants to destroy of the world. However, soon after it casts a spell, it is vulnerably eaten by a pigeon. People find this tragic character quite cute.

II.B.c.ii. **Name**

The wolf's name is Flipper (Fig. 4.43, right), but the image that it is sweating when nervously driving a car is funny.

Fig. 4.42 Example of a character that says "no" but with a soft heart (*Image source* Manga109 dataset, used with permission)

タナベキヨミ短編集・桃山灰神楽
MomoyamaHaikagura
Copyright © Tanabe Kiyomi

藤太参ります！
ToutaMairimasu
Copyright © Saijo Shinji

あくはむ
Akuhamu
Copyright © Arai Satoshi

燃える！お兄さん
MoeruOnisan
Copyright © Sato Tadashi

Fig. 4.43 Examples of characters with personalities/behaviors different from their social status (*left*), name (*middle*), or fame (*right*) (*Image source* Manga109 dataset, used with permission)

II.B.c.iii. **Fame**

The girl on the left of Fig. 4.43 is the daughter of a mafia family who is raised to be quite violent. However, the fact that she cries really hard after loosing a battle makes her a lovely character. Garfield is another example. He is known to be mean, but his fondness for his Teddy bear makes him cute.

II.B.d. **Cute by Appearance–Identity Contrast**

The mismatch between identity and appearance can also result in the sense of cuteness.

II.B.d.i. **Age**

The disparity between a character's physical age (appearance) and mental age (identity) can be a source of cuteness, such as a fairly mature child-looking figure or a character with a full-grown body but a childish mind (Fig. 4.44, left).

うるとら☆イレブン
UltraEleven
Copyright © Yabuno Tenya, Watanabe Tatsuya

空っぽハイスクール
KarappoHighschool
Copyright © Takaguchi Satosumi

Fig. 4.44 Examples of high school male characters that appear like a child (age, *left*) or is shy like a girl (gender, *right*) (*Image source* Manga109 dataset, used with permission)

Fig. 4.45 Examples of devils dressed up in cute (cat and rabbit) costumes (*Image source* Manga109 dataset, used with permission)

てんしのはねとアクマのシッポ
TensiNoHaneToAkumaNoShippo
Copyright © Kiriga Yuki

やさしい悪魔
YasasiiAkuma
Copyright © Hanada Sakumi

II.B.d.ii. Gender (偽娘, 偽郎)

Sometimes people may think characters with certain features of the opposite sex are cute, such as a baby boy dressed in pink (assuming standard twentieth-century color cues) or a young man who is overly shy (Fig. 4.44, right).

II.B.d.iii. Profession

Another common cuteness-evoking appearance-identity discrepancy is associated with profession (role). For examples, the characters dressed up in cat and bunny costumes in Fig. 4.45 are actually devils.

4.2 Strategies of Playing Cute

In real life, people have developed strategies for "cutifying" themselves (a.k.a., playing cute) or a design, usually by changing appearance or performing certain behaviors.

Appearance-based Playing Cute

The simplest way is to wear a costume that is deemed cute. The style of clothing depends on the type of cuteness to apply, such as the bunny girl outfit for sexy cute (Fig. 4.3) versus the mascot-like rabbit suit for animal cute (Figs. 4.36 and 4.45).

Changing shape and proportion of the body and face is another shortcut to cuteness. A good example is Stitch, a popular Disney character. When its mouth is shut, the big ears make Stitch a calm innocent cute animal, like Pikachu. When Stitch shows its sharp teeth, people are supposed to get panicky. However, by giving it a fat round body, big round head, and large eyes, fear is overcome by the sense of cuteness. See Fig. 4.46 for another example. Such strategies are applied on the design of "scary" pumpkin man decorations in Hong Kong Ocean Park in November 2016 (effect similar to Fig. 4.47).

Fig. 4.46 Cute and scary
bunny (Illustration by
Xiaojuan Ma, used with
permission)

Fig. 4.47 Halloween
pumpkin character sticker
(Illustration by Xiaojuan Ma,
used with permission)

Behavior-based Playing Cute

People can create the perception of cuteness by gestures and body movements that
signal naïve, soft, or animal cuteness, such as winking, tilting the head, hands on
chin, hands over the mouth, arms wide open asking for a hug, lifting one leg in the
air, peeking from behind an obstacle, wagging a tail, waving hands like the fortune
cat (招财猫 Maneki Neko 招き猫), *etc*. See Figs. 4.8, 4.15, and 4.16 for examples.

4.3   Higher Level Taxonomical Features of Cuteness

Beyond the detailed list presented above, additional higher level taxonomical categories of cuteness include the following. Each of these provides additional
dimensions by which cuteness products and services can be described, analyzed,
designed, and evaluated.

Evolution of Cuteness

Cuteness-Historical Changes: For example, the evolution of the look of Mickey Mouse, Hello Kitty, Garfield the cat, and other cartoon characters over decades of time.

Cuteness-Social Influence: For example, the Otaku phenomenon, a Japanese term for people with obsessive interests, commonly used for fans of Japanese *animé* and *manga*. See: http://en.wikipedia.org/wiki/Otaku.

Cuteness-Technology Orientation: From just the appearance (*e.g.*, icon design) to more extensive characteristics of functions and services. See Yamaha's Hatsune Miku singing synthesizer https://en.wikipedia.org/wiki/Hatsune_Miku). The Yamaha's Hatsune Miku singing synthesizer enables character designers to design the voice and musical characteristics of the character's speech.

Dependence of Cuteness

We acknowledge this dimension to Wentao Wang of Baidu, who mentions this dimension in his discussions (see Chap. 5) and includes some cuteness concepts in the Baidu user-experience design guidelines (Baidu 2014).

Cuteness-Age Dependence: Baby, child, teenager, senior, *etc.*

Cuteness-Context Dependence: Advertising, education, medical, government, sport, entertainment, *etc.*

Cuteness-Culture Dependence: European, North American, Indian, Asian, Chinese, Japanese, Korean, *etc.*

Cuteness-Education Dependence: Advanced education may reduce sensitivity to cuteness.

Cuteness-Gender Dependence: Men, women, other genders.

Cuteness-Profession Dependence: Designers may be more sensitive.

Media Elements of Cuteness

Cuteness-Medium: Emojis/emoticons, mascots, ACG (animation, comics, games), films, television shows, *etc.*

Cuteness-Appearance: Color, *e.g.*, pink and other pastels), shapes (rounded, blobs), face treatment (baby-like, large eyes), anthropomorphism (*e.g.*, hammers can become human-like characters), expression (hyperbolic, ritualized), *etc.*).

Cuteness-Sound: voice, sound (*e.g.*, *Pikachu*), *etc.* Pikachu are Japanese fictional Pokémon creatures that appear in comics, animations, games, and movies/television. See: https://en.wikipedia.org/wiki/Pokémon_Pikachu.

Cuteness-Language: slangs and symbols, *e.g.*, 萌萌哒 ("so cute," frequently seen in Chinese social media), 么么哒 ("kiss kiss"), the tilde symbol ("~"), *etc.*

Cuteness-Behavior: gesture, posture, *etc.* The term "acting/playing cute" means someone deliberately attracts others by showing off (or pretending) to be cute, such as the leading character in the 2011 movie *Puss in Boots*. The use of *kaomoji* in Japanese social media is another example. See http://kaomoji.ru/en. The Website notes that these emoticons are strongly Japanese and that the Japanese consider the eyes the source or chief denoter of emotion.

Value of Cuteness:

Cuteness-Psychological Value: Keeping people curious, interested, and engaged.

Cuteness-Social Value: Establishing and/or reinforcing social groups and power positions (or powerlessness positions).

Cuteness-Economic Value: Establishing and/or reinforcing brand value.

Cuteness-Culture Value: Establishing and/or reinforcing culture values through cute symbols and cute heros and heroines.

Examples can be found at many different Websites. For examples, see: http://www.56.com/u53/v_MTI5OTE2ODE4.html and http://www.bilibili.com/video/av1701475/.

4.4   Conclusions

This taxonomy is an ongoing project. We expect it to expand and differentiate in detail as more examples become well known to students of cuteness engineering/design and as cuteness expands its role in the ongoing development of products and services.

References

Baidu UX Department (2014) Baidu UX design guidelines (in Chinese). Baidu, Beijing, p 234

Hildebrandt KA, Fitzgerald HE (1979) Adults' perceptions of infant sex and cuteness. Sex Roles 5:471–481

Lorenz K (1971) Part and parcel in animal and human societies. In: Lorenz K (ed) Studies in animal and human behavior, vol 2. Harvard University Press, Cambridge, pp 115–195

Matsui Y, Ito K, Aramaki Y, Yamasaki T, Aizawa K (2015) Sketch-based Manga Retrieval using Manga109 Dataset. arXiv:1510.04389

Chapter 5
Interview with Yuko Yamaguchi
(Hello Kitty Designer)

5.1 Introduction

We conducted an interview with Ms. Yuko Yamaguchi, the third designer to be responsible for Hello Kitty, asking about her approach to "cuteness" regarding the world-famous character design of Hello Kitty (Fig. 5.1).

1. **Personal Background of Ms. Yamaguchi**

Q: In conducting preliminary research for this interview, we discovered that your art teacher in junior high school recommended that you go to an art university. As a student, what sort of future career did you envision for yourself?

Junior High Years

I was in the brass band in junior high school. I actually had no desire to do art, nor did I particularly like it. My art teacher recommended that I pursue a career in design, but I was not sure if he meant fashion design or graphic design. This recommendation actually came during calligraphy class. I was told that I had an outstanding ability to quickly draw Japanese characters. Until then, I was not aware that I had this kind of ability, because I just assumed that everyone could do calligraphy.

At that time, I also created my own original letters, and was unaware that I had the unique ability to draw them quickly. I was thinking that anyone could do it. Back then, calligraphy classes were very rare for junior high school. I think that this particular art teacher was a great teacher in terms of design. He recommended that I should go to a high school, where I could learn from another teacher that he knew.

© Springer International Publishing AG 2017
A. Marcus et al., *Cuteness Engineering*, Springer Series on Cultural Computing,
DOI 10.1007/978-3-319-61961-3_5

Fig. 5.1 Ms. Yuko Yamaguchi, Hello Kitty Designer, Sanrio, Tokyo, Japan

High School Years

Even after I entered high school, I did not particularly like art. I was involved in a lot of activities such as student council and a Committee on Human Rights that was made up of high school students in Kochi Prefecture. I belonged to the art club, and my teacher told me, "If you want to make a name for yourself in Kochi, you need to win a prize at the Kochi Prefecture Exhibition." Later, I went on to win a prize in my first year of high school. The media made a big deal of it because of my age. I appeared on an NHK TV program, and was featured in a big article in *The Kochi Shimbun* newspaper too. I received an honorable mention in my second year, when my teacher told me, "You can't make a name for yourself with an honorable mention. You've got to win the big prize." Then, I felt that winning a prize was my only option. In my third year, I won a Certificate of Merit, which is the prize above the honorable mention. So, in the end, I feel like I was able to achieve one of the goals of my high school career. However, even then, I did not have any idea about what sort of career I wanted to pursue.

Moving to Tokyo and University Years

Since junior high school I had wanted to live in Tokyo, and I was sure I could find something if I went to Tokyo. There were a lot of things I wanted to do. For example, I was a member of the brass band in junior high school, but actually I wanted to play basketball. But at the time, I was learning piano and I feared that I might hurt my fingers and gave up the idea of joining the basketball team. But it was always in the back of my mind that if I moved to Tokyo for university, then I would definitely play basketball.

After high school, I entered Joshibi University of Art and Design and joined the basketball club for all four years. In my university years, my parents were not providing financial support and I did not have much money. I had to work part-time to cover my living expenses. My life consisted of going to class in the morning, playing basketball in the afternoon, and working at night.

Employment and Sanrio

When it was time to look for a job, I was unable to decide what sort of career I should pursue, so I visited many companies. From childhood, I had loved collecting character goods, and I thought of visiting companies that handle characters. But, at that time, there were just a few companies that would hire a woman living on her own. It was generally thought that a woman living on her own applying to companies would be a waste of time.

It was then that I found the job listing from Sanrio. It said the company was "looking for youths who are confident in their physical strength." Because I had been playing basketball for four years, I had confidence in my physical strength. However, I had no idea what sort of company Sanrio was. Naturally, I knew about Hello Kitty, but I did not connect this with Sanrio. I knew about the Gift Gate shop located in the Adhoc Shinjuku Building, but I did not know that Sanrio ran it.

I had no idea what Sanrio did, but I went to the company information session. The founder and CEO (Shintaro Tsuji, who is still the CEO) came out and introduced the company. I visited many companies and usually it was the human resources manager that introduced the company. None of the other companies had their CEO come out and talk to us. What really moved me about Sanrio's information session were Tsuji's words, "Our company plans to try our hand at a lot of different businesses." I was shocked when he told us, "Our company is divided into sales, management, design, and other categories. However, I want each of you to think about what you want to do." I felt that a CEO such as Mr. Tsuji would not likely say something like "designers should only draw."

I did not like drawing all day long. In fact, drawing was something that did not appeal to me. I just wanted to get it over and done with as soon as possible. I liked thinking up ideas, but I always felt that the time I spent expressing those ideas was a waste of time. I used to wonder if there was a more efficient way. This is because we did not have computers back then. In other words, all the drawing was done by hand. At my art university, there were a lot of people who liked the idea of becoming designers, or enjoyed the time they spent drawing. Similarly, there were a lot of Sanrio designers who enjoyed the time they spent drawing, but that was not true in my case. When I heard Mr. Tsuji speak at the information session, I felt that there was no need for me to become a designer if I joined Sanrio. I thought I could just become a salesperson or an office worker.

2. Joining Sanrio and Becoming a Character Designer for Hello Kitty

Q: How did you become a character designer after joining Sanrio?

Early Days at Sanrio

In the end, I was one of ten people hired for creative positions. Half a year later, we were called together in a room to take an aptitude test. This test determined whether we would become planners or designers. Half a year after the aptitude test, we were called one at a time to talk with the department director, who informed us whether we would be planners or designers. On that day, everyone came out of the room crying. I asked them what happened, and they told me, "I was told that I'm going to be a planner." At Sanrio, those who create the characters are the stars, and many people want to be a designer.

I was told I would be a designer and assigned to be a newly formed non-character group. Of course, Sanrio did not want to lose customers to the competition. As such, the aim of this group was to create non-character designs that would appeal to children after they had outgrown characters like Hello Kitty or Little Twin Stars (Fig. 5.2). At that time, character products were seen as being for children in elementary school or below. This design team was tasked with creating products for customers above that age range. Fresh Punch (Fig. 5.3) was a non-character product that we created at the time, and it is still on the market today. Then we started to design accessories for Patty and Jimmy (Fig. 5.4). We redesigned them without the characters themselves. That was how Fresh Punch originated.

Becoming a Hello Kitty Character Designer

Eventually, Hello Kitty sales began to decrease little by little. From my standpoint as a third party, it seemed natural that Patty and Jimmy and Hello Kitty sales would drop. At that time, there were about 60 designers at Sanrio, and there was a lack of communication among them.

Until then, I had never spoken with the designers who drew Patty and Jimmy, Hello Kitty, or Little Twin Stars. In addition, characters had the perception of being for children, and the public had begun to lose interest in these characters. The second Hello Kitty designer quit her job after sales started to fall, and I thought that there would not be any more designers assigned to Hello Kitty. Patty and Jimmy did not get a third character designer, and I thought that Sanrio would stop making Hello Kitty products. However, CEO Tsuji told the designers: "Hello Kitty was a character created as a symbol of friendship. We can't allow her to disappear from the market. We will choose a third character designer." I never imagined that I would be tasked with Hello Kitty designs. All of a sudden, it was decided that we would be choosing the third Hello Kitty character designer, and the department director instructed me to design and present a new Hello Kitty. At the time, I thought, "Do I really have to do this?" Later, all of the designers drew their own Hello Kitty designs and presented them to the department director. Then, he told me, that I was to be in charge of "growing" Hello Kitty. That is how I became the third designer for Hello Kitty (Fig. 5.5).

Fig. 5.2 Little Twin Stars (Copyright © 1976, 2017, by Sanrio Co., Ltd., used with permission)

Q: What sort of drawing did you create at that time?

The title of my drawing was "Hello Kitty's first grand piano" (Fig. 5.4). I have always thought it very strange that Hello Kitty never actually played the piano although she used to say that her dream was to become a pianist. In fact, my parents wanted me to become a pianist or, at least, a music teacher. But I could never understand the fun of playing the piano. Even in my case, our family had a grand piano at home. So I thought that surely there would be a piano in the house of Hello Kitty, who aspired to be a professional pianist. During my presentation, I told the following story.

> Hello Kitty was timidly playing her first grand piano. Her father George, who bought the piano, was boasting about how great it is, while her mother Mary felt a great deal of pride in him. Her younger twin sister Mimmy wanted to grow up and become a bride. She didn't

Fig. 5.3 Fresh Punch (Copyright © 1981, 2017 by Sanrio Co., Ltd.; used with permission)

take piano lessons, and didn't want to be a pianist, but she was still a little jealous of her sister Hello Kitty.

After I told this story to the department director, he said, "You're in charge of nurturing Hello Kitty."

Q: Do you know what kind of drawings the other designers created?

They showed me the drawings of the other designers after the decision had been made. Many of them drew Hello Kitty in a style akin to Andy Warhol, or changed the design to look like a graphic design. I know the other designers had spent a lot of time and effort on their drawings, but I did not like spending a lot of time on the drawing. I spent very little time on the drawing. I did not like drawing very much, so I did not use a pencil for drawing the draft, and went straight to my pens. I also wanted to save time for coloring the drawing, so I just applied Pantone Overlay sheets, which are similar to screen tone sheets that were popular at the time.

Q: Given that, why do you think your work was so well received?

I am sure it was because of the story. Everyone else was trying to change the graphics, but I chose a different approach. In addition, Hello Kitty had always been standing or sitting with her legs to one side. There were no pictures like mine

Fig. 5.4 Patty & Jimmy (Copyright © 1976, 2017 by Sanrio Co. Ltd.; used with permission)

Fig. 5.5 Hello Kitty's first grand piano (Copyright © 1976, 2017 by Sanrio, Co., Ltd.; used with permission)

featuring her drawn viewed from a slightly oblique perspective. On top of that, they had apparently never drawn Hello Kitty's face, and had only drawn her body from the neck down. But if you don't draw the face, then you can't express movement, and you can't show the emotion. I decided to draw Hello Kitty at an angle because she couldn't play the piano by just standing or sitting with her legs to her side. It would be unnatural for her to be sitting with her legs to her side, and it would look as if she were sitting next to the toy piano. So I decided to draw her with an all-new design, including her face, from a different angle.

Q: Was it difficult to draw Hello Kitty given that you were asked to do so out of the blue?

No, not really. I was very good at reproducing things that already existed. I have never traced another drawing. If, for example, you were to test me right now by asking me to suddenly draw something without an example, I would not be able to do that. However, I would be able to draw it once I had seen an example. I think maybe I can reproduce things just like a camera.

Q: You said that at that time among Sanrio characters you preferred Little Twin Stars to Hello Kitty. What appealed to you about Little Twin Stars?

I liked Little Twin Stars because they had a story. Hello Kitty left me with the impression of a "flat cat." It was appealing that Little Twin Stars existed in a three-dimensional not a two-dimensional space, and that many colors were used with them. In the early years, only a limited number of colors could be used for Hello Kitty. But with Little Twin Stars, you could use pastel and night sky colors, and I liked that with them you could also use a wide range of art supplies, including colored pencils and pastels.

3. After Becoming the Third Hello Kitty Character Designer

Q: What did you do after becoming Hello Kitty's character designer, and what were you thinking while you were doing it?

Initially, I thought I should try to make some allies. Within the company where most people thought there was no need to create products for characters that didn't sell well, I thought I'd have a hard time finding any like-minded individuals. I thought I needed the allies to create products, so the first thing I did was to ask my colleagues why customers who bought Hello Kitty products stopped buying them. Sanrio did not have a marketing department capable of doing the market research. But I thought it would be embarrassing to visit stores and ask customers what they thought.

It was then that I had an idea. I saw a new singer doing a marketing campaign in front of the record store, and I immediately thought that was the solution. The singer was standing on a beer crate, passing out fliers and shouting: "Please buy my records!" I thought people would come and I could ask many questions about Hello Kitty products if I positioned myself at the storefront and handed out drawings of Hello Kitty with my autograph. At first, we did not call it a signing session, but that was the beginning of our autograph sessions.

Things Learned From Customer Comments

At that time, we had a great deal of franchise stores, and we obtained permission from the franchise owners and asked people's opinions at the stores. Gradually, I learned why people stopped buying. There were two cases. In one case, customers had a lot of Hello Kitty products and to them she had become stale. Also, many people compared Hello Kitty to Little Twin Stars. People liked the cute pastel colors of Little Twin Stars. They loved the sibling love of the twins, and thought that their star-shaped accessories were cute. These were all the things that Hello Kitty lacked. This made me think that we needed to try various new approaches with Hello Kitty. This got me thinking that Hello Kitty needed to be everyone's idol, someone asked me "Does Hello Kitty wear only one outfit? That is not very fashionable." This made me think that we needed to give her various outfits. Just when I was thinking that Hello Kitty should like the same things that everyone else likes, there was a teddy bear boom in Japan. I started to draw Hello Kitty with her teddy bear, to show that she also likes teddy bears.

Experiences in America

Around that time, our American subsidiary, Sanrio, Inc., was launching a design office, and I spent a year working there in 1984. Since I was going to be out of touch with Japan, I felt that it was the right time to start building a portfolio of Hello Kitty illustrations, so I drew a lot of them. At that time, we didn't have computers, and international calls were very expensive. I also couldn't get Japanese magazines there, and the only Japanese TV programs I could watch were NHK Taiga Drama series and the annual Kohaku year-end song competition. So, I was not watching much TV. Back then in America, there was an even bigger teddy bear boom than in Japan, and I saw a few stores carrying nothing but teddy bears. That was when I created the story about Hello Kitty and her teddy bear. The teddy bear I drew was just a plain old bear. He did not even have a name. Later I gave him the name Tiny Chum (Fig. 5.6), and created the following story.

> Tiny Chum is a boy who lived in Hello Kitty's neighborhood. He likes Hello Kitty, and wears the same ribbon as Hello Kitty even though he's a boy. But his parents moved to New York, so Tiny Chum ended up going to live at the home of his idol Hello Kitty.

That was the idea I had as I drew more and more illustrations. A year later, after coming back to Japan, we released the Tiny Chum series of products in the fall of 1985.

Tiny Chum Series is a Hit

In the fall of 1985, the Tiny Chum series sold extremely well, and Hello Kitty became Sanrio's top-selling character for the first time. Since then, Hello Kitty has been our company's top-selling character. The Tiny Chum series sold well not just in Japan, but also in the United States. Many people likely learned about Hello Kitty through the Tiny Chum series. However, the products sold in America were imported directly from Japan and the price was triple that in Japan. These prices were so high that only celebrities could afford them.

Fig. 5.6 Tiny Chum (Copyright © 1985, 2017 by Sanrio Co., Ltd.; used with permission)

I think the teddy bear is a good example of how people around the world can prefer the same thing. The teddy bear was first created in Germany, and the British started buying more and more of them. Then, one of them was given to a US president that was when they gained the nickname "teddy bear"—then it became a big hit in the US. Later, after it came to Japan, the Japanese fell in love with it as well.

[**Editor's Note**: "The **teddy bear** is named after U.S. President Theodore "**Teddy**" Roosevelt. In 1902, President Roosevelt participated in a **bear**-hunting trip in Mississippi. While hunting, Roosevelt declared the behavior of the other hunters "unsportsmanlike" after he refused to kill a **bear** they had captured." (According to http://wonderopolis.org/wonder/how-did-the-teddy-bear-get-its-name. Checked on 26 May 2017.)]

Q: When creating the story of Hello Kitty, were you consciously influenced by foreign cultures?

When Hello Kitty first appeared in the early 1970s, there were many Anglophiles in Japan. At the very beginning, there was a story that Hello Kitty was born in London, England. When I started drawing Hello Kitty in the 1980s, Japanese girls had all shifted their aspirations to America, so I decided to adopt the elements of American culture. As a result, the number of England-esque drawings decreased, but I think Japanese people weren't very aware of Hello Kitty having been born in England, although her profile states that she was born in a suburb of London, England. Today, the Japanese don't really romanticize any single country, and the background of drawings aren't specifically England or America.

4. **Expanding the Target Demographic via Autograph Sessions and Style Guides**

Q: After that, how did you go about broadening the target demographic?

Hello Kitty was originally aimed at elementary school children, but from 1987 we targeted high school students. At first, we focused on stationery products, but we later introduced fashion items such as T-shirts, hats, and shoes aimed at high school students. When we started making items other than stationery, I incorporated the latest fashion trends. If monochrome was in fashion, I used monochrome elements in my designs. If tartan patterns were in fashion, I used them. We made many different sets of things that high school students would buy. High school students are physically adults, so their bodies are much larger than elementary school children. So, whether it was for T-shirts or swim rings, we made them in different sizes: smaller sizes for elementary school children and larger sizes for high school students. The Pink Quilt Series (Fig. 5.7) sold well with working women.

We started making mobile phone cases (Fig. 5.8) because at the time everyone started carrying mobile phones. They sold so well that practically everyone you would see on the train had one. I think that people at that time just wanted to show off that they had a mobile phone.

Fig. 5.7 Pink Quilt Series (Copyright © 2017 by Sanrio Co., Ltd.; used with permission)

Fig. 5.8 Pink Quilt Mobile
Phone Case (Copyright ©
2017 by Sanrio Co., Ltd.;
used with permission)

Subsequently, we introduced bath and toiletry goods aimed at working women living alone, but housewives also started buying them. Next, we created kitchen utensils and living room items for housewives around 1997.

Around this time in Japan, a lot of adults were buying pink Hello Kitty products, so people called it the "Hello Kitty Boom." However, many of these customers were people who purchased the Hello Kitty teddy bear series in 1984 as children. Outside Japan, celebrities bought teddy bear products that appeared on the market in 1984 and the Tiny Chum Series appearing in 1985. I think these people, who bought these products as children, started buying Hello Kitty after 2000. That was the start of the Hello Kitty Boom. Then it started selling well in America and European countries, and Hello Kitty found fans worldwide.

Q: Where did you get the information that Hello Kitty was selling well with working women and housewives?

I obtained all the relevant information from autograph sessions. I do about 40 autograph sessions per year. Initially, the people who came to the sessions were elementary school children, but I saw that the demographics of the people were rapidly changing. I tried adding new story elements based on the comments of people at autograph sessions. People all loved to hear about the behind-the-scenes stories, with questions like "Does Hello Kitty have a boyfriend?" or "What's her blood type?" That's what prompted me to create her boyfriend Dear Daniel (Fig. 5.9) in 1999. Before then, she did not have a boyfriend, and when we created products featuring a boy and girl pair, such as with *Hinamatsuri*[1] dolls, we had her sister Mimmy sometimes fill in for a boy. Creating Dear Daniel was very convenient for goods like that. Before that, the wedding cake dolls we made featured Hello Kitty by herself in a wedding dress. Later, we were able to create a pair featuring Dear Daniel in a tuxedo next to her.

[**Editor's note**: *[1]Hinamatsuri* is a doll festival that is celebrated every year on March 3 in Japan. It is an occasion to pray for young girls' growth and happiness, and most families with girls display a pair of dolls with doll servants on a terrace. Dolls for the festival are called *Hina-ningyo*.]

At one point I was thinking that maybe fans also wanted her to marry her boyfriend Dear Daniel and have children, but that was not the case. When I asked fans if Hello Kitty should marry Dear Daniel at an autograph session, the answer was, "Absolutely not." There are fans of both. Fans of Dear Daniel think of Hello Kitty as the rival, while Hello Kitty fans think "I'll never let her marry Dear Daniel"

Fig. 5.9 Hello Kitty and Boyfriend Dear Daniel (Copyright © 1976, 1999, 2017 by Sanrio Co., Ltd.; used with permission)

or "Hello Kitty having children is unimaginable." I think autograph sessions are the only place I can get information like this.

Even if we were able to spend money on a marketing survey, I wouldn't trust the results. This is because surveys are made up of only "yes" or "no" questions, and you can't meet the respondents. Personally, I think it is better for me to talk with people in person at autograph sessions, asking questions like, "OK, what do you want me to do?" I spend a few minutes writing each autograph, so that I can talk with them during that time.

Q: What age group has the most Hello Kitty fans?

Now, people in their thirties and forties are common at autograph sessions. It isn't that we are always aiming at people in their teens and twenties. We are always thinking about people who tell us they like Hello Kitty. If this happens for the people in their thirties and forties, then we'll focus on people in their thirties and forties. These days, people in their teens and twenties wear relatively plain clothing, and I suspect that they don't like cute things that much. Even so, we're also trying to attract interest from children in their teens and younger. Basically, fans in their thirties and their children use our products. Many fans in their thirties have friends who are also mothers. As a result, if any of them buy a product, it spreads from there. In fact, there are also many parents who come to autograph sessions with children. Couples also come. More men are starting to come too, and they are usually younger, in their twenties or so.

When I met the K-pop group TVXQ (Tong Vfang Xien Qi) before they became famous, they did not seem to be interested in Hello Kitty. But a few years later, when they became popular in Japan, they jumped at the chance for a collaborative initiative with Hello Kitty when we made the proposal. This led to the Hello Kitty hairclip used by a member of the group called Junsu during a concert, and it sold well with their fans.

I have been able to meet many different people from entertainers to regular people, and I have connections with people of all ages. I get information from many different types of people.

Q: What sort of marketing strategy did you use with Hello Kitty?

None in particular. We let it flow naturally. This is because our company does not have a marketing department, and for some reason we never made one.

Q: I have heard that you have a style guide for Hello Kitty character designs. Can you describe it?

The style guides are something that we create when we try to expand into foreign countries. The content of each style guide is completely different. Our first subsidiary was established in the United States. However, each country has its own style guide. Japan also has its own style guide. While the basic designs of the faces do not change, each country has its own preference for designs and colors.

Since we have a lot of licensees, we provide them with a style guide when they sign a licensing agreement. However, it is not written in stone. When they want to use a different design, we essentially just ask them to seek approval for the new designs. When a licensee has an idea, we fix it for them, reject it, or give it the OK. Our licensees provide us with a constant supply of new ideas this way. The style guide contains basic illustrations of Hello Kitty, and licensees are using the style guide to propose ways to customize them or different directions they wish to develop with the character worldview, which we check and approve.

5. Concept of Cuteness

Q: Did you or Sanrio consciously think of the concept of "cuteness" when developing Hello Kitty?

No. I think the word "cute" is an afterthought. Originally, we were not talking about cuteness. It was added later because of today's culture of cuteness.

Q: Can you tell us of any stories where you were conscious of something "cute"?

The first time I heard the word "cute" (*kawaii*) was from the designer Rei Yanagawa. I think she was the first person who used the word "cute," in that way. I recall her saying: "Strawberries are cute, aren't they?"

   I've loved fashion since junior high school, and I love collecting clothes, although I never thought of becoming a fashion designer. In my junior and senior high school days, I admired the designer Rei Yanagawa. She always asked the question: "Is it wrong to have a desire to wear cute clothes after you've grown up?" However, it was considered crazy for an adult to wear clothes with lace trimmings, for example. However, she created a fashion brand called MILK, saying, "It's ok for girls to say that they always want to wear cute clothes!" At that time, many entertainers wore MILK clothes, but they were very expensive. I wanted to buy MILK clothes when I went to Tokyo. But I couldn't afford them. Now, MILK is not such an expensive brand any more, but when the brand was still relatively new, it was like buying Chanel. I couldn't even afford a T-shirt. Socks were all I could afford.

Q: What kind of things do you feel are "cute?"

In terms of fruits, I think strawberries are absolutely cute. I prefer both real strawberries and the concept of strawberries. Cherries are also cute. As for colors, I would say pink and red are cute colors.

   Lace is also cute. Girls just love lace. I think we yearn to wear clothes with lace and frills so that we can wear what princesses used to wear in the past. We can feel like princesses ourselves. I believe this is the influence of picture books. Most things that young girls desire are cute, aren't they?

Q: Do you think the shape and size of things matter when it comes to cuteness?

I think things with soft edges are probably cute in general. When talking about cute flowers, daisies and tulips both have soft qualities. I think beauty and cuteness are different things. Few people might refer to a lily as cute, and angular things are rarely referred to as "cute," so I think there is a relationship between soft edges and cuteness. I personally do not think that the size of an object matters.

Q: Which characters do you think are cute?

My favorite characters are Mickey Mouse and Snoopy. They are the kings of cute. I also like Peko-chan. Although I do not like the job of drawing characters, I've liked collecting character merchandise since I was a child. When I was collecting vintage merchandise, I loved researching the roots of a character—such as who drew it and how it found fans and spread around the world. I think Mickey Mouse, Snoopy, and Peko-chan are the three cutest characters. I also drew Peko-chan of Fujiya as part of my job, so my feeling about her is not quite the same as for Mickey Mouse and Snoopy. They have a long history and I respect them as characters.

Fujiya is a good company, and they know that I like Peko-chan. About 20 years ago they came to Sanrio and asked if Sanrio would like to release products featuring Peko-chan exclusively. They told me that I could draw all the illustrations, and I did.

6. Relationship with Hello Kitty

Q: What does Hello Kitty mean to you?

For me, Hello Kitty is a business partner, and I do not consider her to be cute. I don't even really like her. I never wore Hello Kitty clothes or used Hello Kitty accessories like other people do. I am not her fan, but I am her character designer. If I loved Hello Kitty, I might want to completely redesign her in a new way. But if I did that, she would no longer be the Hello Kitty that we all know. This is business, not self-expression for me. I draw her in the way that people want her to be. Hello Kitty is just a business partner I work with and so our lives are intertwined.

Right now, I am holding a Hello Kitty pen and notepad, but that is because I'm in the office. I do not have any Hello Kitty products at home as they make me feel like she is forcing me to work constantly.

Q: If you were not involved in designing Hello Kitty, what sort of impression would you have of her?

I'm not sure, but because Hello Kitty hasn't been around me for that long, I may not be interested in buying Hello Kitty merchandise. The merchandise I am collecting now is not new Mickey Mouse and Snoopy items, but some of the first products ever made. Compared to Mickey Mouse and Snoopy, the 40-year history of Hello Kitty is relatively short. Well, I might be interested in getting the first Hello Kitty product, "the petite purse" (Fig. 5.10) that is kept in Sanrio's safe, but that is the only one in the world. Of course, it would be impossible to obtain it.

Q: After working with Hello Kitty for 36 years, how have your relationship with and feelings toward her changed?

I wanted to be a friend with Hello Kitty and we were friends at first. But after Hello Kitty became Sanrio's top-selling character, I felt like she was not so much a friend,

Fig. 5.10 The Petite Purse (Copyright © 2017 by Sanrio Co., Ltd.; used with permission)

but more an extension of myself. When Hello Kitty became popular around the world in 2000, I decided that she's not a part of me, but rather that we are purely business partners. So, we have been business partners for 16 years.

Q: Where would you like to take Hello Kitty in the future?

Up until 2006, my energies were entirely focused on Hello Kitty. However, about 10 years ago I was asked to take care of other characters as well. So for the last 10 years, I have been in a position where I have to promote other characters as well, and the way I interact with Hello Kitty has changed. It is as if I am running a talent agency, and Hello Kitty is just one of my stable of stars. I can't afford to look after her exclusively, although I would like to try to combine her as a package deal with other characters. In way resembling a talent agency trying to get work for new talent, I consider how to use Hello Kitty to increase the popularity of other characters. At the same time, I do worry about the issue of overlapping the characters. In order for a character to survive, you can't make the same things along the same lines. You can't allow other characters to do the same thing that Hello Kitty has done in the past. I think it is imperative to ensure the individuality of each character, whether it is their color, clothes or something else.

Fig. 5.11 The images show the history of Hello Kitty since 1974 (Copyright © 1976, 2017 by Sanrio Co., Ltd.; used with permission)

Post-Script: Visual History of Hello Kitty Since 1974

See Fig. 5.11.

Postscript: Hello Kitty Visual History Since 1974

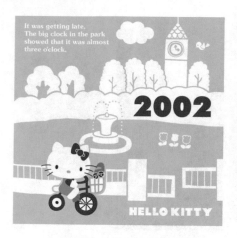

© 1976, 2017 SANRIO CO., LTD.

Chapter 6
Cuteness Design: Interview with Wentao Wang, Senior User-Experience Designer, Baidu, Beijing, China

6.1 Introduction

The following interview with Wentao Wang, Senior User-Experience Designer at Baidu, Beijing, China (see Fig. 6.1) occurred via Skype on 22 November 2015 by book co-author Prof. Xiaojuan Ma, Assistant Professor, HCI Program, Department of Computer Science and Engineering, University of Science and Technology, Hong Kong, China.

6.2 Background/Personal Questions

Q: In this interview, we want to focus on learning about how you made your user-experience (UX) design decisions, how these decisions may have changed over time, and what factors contributed to these changes.
How long have you been a graphic designer, visual designer, or interaction designer? Please specify which role(s) you have had.

I've been with Baidu for 8–9 years. Currently, I am the senior design manager, with a team of 30+ visual and interaction designers. Our team belongs to the Baidu UX department (200+ designers).
We're responsible for designing the interaction logic and branding (logo, mascot, interface, style, color scheme, *etc.*) for both PC and mobile products.

Q: How did you learn to become a designer?

I received a Master's degree in HCI [human-computer interaction] from the University of Michigan. I did UX design at Oracle in California before joining Baidu.

© Springer International Publishing AG 2017
A. Marcus et al., *Cuteness Engineering*, Springer Series on Cultural Computing,
DOI 10.1007/978-3-319-61961-3_6

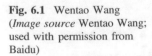

Fig. 6.1 Wentao Wang
(*Image source* Wentao Wang;
used with permission from
Baidu)

Q: What kind of designs are you creating (*e.g.*, domains, styles, target audience, content types, *etc.*)?

There are three kinds of design challenges, with two kinds of styles. Design Challenge 1 is Baidu branding (visual identification). Design Challenge 2 is product style, such as the Baidu stock market manager for the Web or the H5 for mobile. This app is built on Baidu big-data mining, with database intelligent systems, not expert systems Style means: technology, intelligence, big data, and professional qualities. Finally, there is Design Challenge 3: Cross-platform consistency.

Q: What is your experience with, responsibility for, or focus on cuteness, if any?

I have experience with cuteness in mascot design. My history is bound up in Baidu's historic trends. All products and services are becoming more convenient. Users are getting younger and younger. Technologies are meant to bring convenience to everyday life, such as online-to-offline applications. Recall Baidu's slogan: Connect users and services. This slogan implies that all products and services are not too cool or too hard-to-get, but are kind and sweet. Cuteness to us is a good tactic, and outcome is quite promising.

6.3   Cuteness-Related Questions

Q: In this section, we would like to find out about techniques to depict cuteness as well as the conventions commonly adopted by designers. What does cuteness mean in your professional role(s)?

At Baidu, we have attempted [to design in] cuteness, and the results have been been very successful.

We originally did not even think about cuteness. We just knew certain styles would appeal to different people. We have designed five figures for the Baidu mascot: One leading role (welcomed and easily acceptable by all) plus four supporting roles (with very distinct personalities, each of which may be preferred only by a certain subgroup of people). This approach is to address the long-tail problem, that is, appealing to many customers who use only a few of Baidu's products and services.

Q: What is your interpretation of cuteness in design?

Cuteness is not always appropriate. Cuteness should be used according to the profiles and needs of the target audience and characteristics of the product. More cuteness in cases such as photo-modification and entertainment apps; less cuteness in business, financial, and professional apps, such as the stock market app I just mentioned.

Q: What are the common scenarios or applications in design to which cuteness is applied?

We apply them to mascot figures, logos, user interfaces, error messages, welcome pages, PR, icons, widgets, fonts, colors, *etc*. Especially, we adjust cuteness to the theme of various traditional Chinese festivals or events, such as Chinese New Year, Teachers' Day, *etc*.

Q: What do you think of the cuteness phenomenon in design in general? To your knowledge, what is its history and future trend?

There seem to be two trends of increasing use of cuteness in design: (1) for Internet design (in both China and US), for online-to-offline kinds of products and services that are closer and closer to everyday life. (2) human/pet-like designs that are a reflection of the philosophy of Zhong Yong (中庸, meaning being in the middle). Cuteness is not appropriate for everything, especially given finer and finer user classifications or distinctions among user profiles and very vertical applications (for example, definitely not for Oracle products like CRM, ERP). The concept of cuteness sometimes is not very massive or concrete or noticeable. It can be expressed by very small and subtle features, that is, not very tangible details, such as its use in a progress bar, transition animations, *etc*.

Q: What are the major or most potent cute features commonly expressed in design? What are the graphic means to depict cuteness? Are there any conventions in the use of shapes, texture, lines, symbols, colors, and other visual effects to help depicting cuteness? If so, where did those conventions come from?

Cuteness can be depicted by many different kinds of visual techniques, such as alignment layout (irregular), contrast, visual focus, color (warm, high saturation, a bit gray, contrast between bright color and background), line (curves, round corners), texture (not flat, shadows, bold lines, gradations)… The best practices are in Japan.

Q: Are there any fixed templates or rules for how to show cuteness in terms of character design, graphic design, and user-interface design? If so, could you show us some examples?

There aren't templates or rules yet. If a template comes out, it probably will go a bit too far. It will restrict designers' creativity.

Q: Are there any changes in the ways to visualize cuteness over the years?

Yes, cuteness has been affected by two factors: (1) a trend in overall design style, which can be reflected by the evolution of animation (all about cuteness, but the style is changing); (2) change of media: from paper-based media, such as posters, to digital and electronic and computer-based physical platforms.

6.4   Sociocultural Differences-Related Questions

Q: In this section, we are interested in seeking information regarding the possible socio-cultural differences that may influence the creation of designs and the way readers from different background may interpret them.

Are culture-wide acknowledged metaphors (e.g., from idioms) being used in depicting cuteness in design? If you are aware of such phenomena, could you give us some examples? Do you think readers can recognize and understand these metaphorical representations instantly? Accurately?

Some are commonly perceived as cute regardless of the culture, such as a little baby, husky creatures, *etc.* Others are perceived differently. For example, the Chinese consider a dragon to be a good symbol, while Western people think it is a monster. American people think Shrek is cute (with a big belly), but it is disliked by many Chinese people.

Usually, something round with fewer corners is considered cute, such as the Baidu bear (Fig. 6.2). Alibaba Group's TMALL cat mascot (Fig. 6.3) is an exception with a square face, but it has huge eyes.

Fig. 6.2 Baidu bear (Copyrighted by Baidu, used with permission from Baidu)

Fig. 6.3 Mascot of Alibaba Group's TMALL Platform (*Image Source* Tmall.com, copyright 2015, used with permission)

Baozou manhua's cuteness is not because of the face but the very unique, strong personality (rarely seen in real life, but it feels so true) (see Fig. 6.4).

Another example is Hui Tai Lang (a wolf character in a popular Chinese cartoon). He is the "bad guy" but many people like him for his cute personality (*e.g.*, afraid of his wife).

Fig. 6.4 *Baozou* manhhua character (Illustration by Xiaojuan Ma, used with permission)

Q: Are culture-specific elements commonly used in cuteness depiction, *e.g.*, certain imagery, icons, or colors?

It's hard to tell for some, in my experience. Here are the groupings I usually would consider as separate culture-specific areas for cuteness depiction:

- China (mainland)
- East Asia
- Europe
- Hong Kong
- Japan
- Korea, South
- Taiwan
- US
- Western.

The definition of cuteness depends on values and how one perceives and understands the world. For example, American people thought Shrek's overweight fat belly and slow movement to be slow-witted 呆萌 cute, while Chinese people look at his eyes, ears, and big teeth and think he is ugly.

Q: Do different readers interpret cuteness differently?

Gender: Yes. Females have lower bars and are more sensitive. There is some [male] bias that cuteness is a bit "girly."

Age: Yes. For example, Baidu people like to travel with the Baidu bear mascot and take photos with it. People born in the 70s like to take photos at famous locations such as Times square, the White House, *etc.*; those born in the 80s like to take the bear to white-water rafting and sky diving; and those born in the 90s like to take bikini pictures with the bear resting on their chests.

Education: Yes. Those with higher education (*e.g.*, Ph.D., undergraduate, or community college degrees) seem less sensitive, more logical, more serious.

Cultural background: Yes.
Visual literacy: Yes
Language: Yes
Profession: Yes. Designers, sales people (who have more interactions with other people) versus engineers.
Financial status: Yea. One needs to be without serious financial concerns to enjoy or appreciate cuteness. But the correlation is not simply linear.

Q: What are the social-psychological-economic reasons behind the cuteness phenomenon? What is the social-psychological-economic impact of the cuteness phenomenon?

There seem to be several factors. The most important social, psychological, and economic reason seems to boil down to one concept: People are not willing to grow up.
Also important: Zhong Yong's principles:
Staying in the middle, being easily forgivable.
Technologies' exponential growth and development: This leads to products/ services becoming too cold/distant. For example, people are afraid of AI [artificial intelligence] and robots or the scenes depicted in sci-fii movies. Technology growth means there are fewer places to express emotions.
Cuteness introduces life-like feelings and lowers the bar to get to know and appreciate technologies. Cuteness leads to the understanding that technological things can be warm and kind, and can solve everyday problems.

Q: Do you think that the Internet is reducing the differences of cuteness among different cultures and countries?

Yes. People have equal opportunities to obtain and share information. They can better understand and respect each other's cultures. Their aesthetics, philosophies, and values are more compatible. However, it is gradual process with small quantitative changes.

Q: Or, do you think that young people world-wide, born after 1990, have very different attitudes, expectations, or preferences in regard to the use of cuteness in products and services, in advertising, and in user-interfaces in particular?

No…and Yes.
No, in that a certain perception of cuteness does not change with age or generation. For example, in the US, kids below 10 years of age generally believe in Santa Claus, and they will put out stockings. Adults know the truth, but as parents, they tend to protect their kids from the reality. It is something that won't change as one ages.
Yes, in a way that it changes with the era. Cuteness will become more and more commercialized and will spread to a wider variety of businesses. An example is the toy market (with intellectual property protection of cute designs). Many popular cartoon characters, such as Hello Kitty (see Fig. 6.5), Xi Yang Yang and Hui Tai

Lang, and Ali the fox have their own accessories, toys, stationery, entertainment products, *etc.*

It is a kind of branding. An example is Disney (*e.g.*, the super heroes after Disney purchased Marvel).

Q: Thanks for your time and comments. I appreciate your generosity in agreeing to this interview.

You are most welcome. I am glad to have an occasion to comment.

Chapter 7
Conclusions

The importance of cuteness in the design of products and services worldwide has increased significantly over the past several decades, making it imperative that engineers and designers, analysts and evaluators, teachers and students of many professions pay more attention to this subject.

The history of cuteness in diverse cultures is a subject worthy of deeper study. We have shown two examples, in Chaps. 2 and 3, for Japan and China, which provide rich, detailed, and complex paths.

In addition, the taxonomy of cuteness is an ongoing inquiry that bears further analysis, which may give rise to pattern analysis and pattern collections, much like the manga database that provided a strong basis for examples in Chap. 4.

Finally, we have provided two interviews with working designers that provide insight into their philosophy, principles, and working methods. Further studies of professionals in multiple countries and cultures will, in the future, be helpful to a wide variety of readers.

Although one can only speculate at this point, the authors believes the characteristics and issues described here can provide guidance and stimulation to others who may be able to research topics more thoroughly and provide further insights, leading to design guidelines for specific audiences, consumers, cultures, and contexts.

We hope we have contributed usably, usefully, and appealingly to the exploration of cuteness.

© Springer International Publishing AG 2017
A. Marcus et al., *Cuteness Engineering*, Springer Series on Cultural Computing,
DOI 10.1007/978-3-319-61961-3_7

Index

A

Acute, 33
Adam Cheyer, 25
Affection, 35
Age-jou, 49
Akhenaten, 1
Akihabara, 55
Alice, 45
Ama-Loli, 46
An-an, 40
Angelic Pretty, 46
Animal cute, 99, 115
Animé, 41, 55, 56
Animé Ambassador project, 41
Appeal, 41
Appearance, 11, 19
Ashamed, 37
Attractive, 49
Attractiveness, 41
Audrey Hepburn, 58
Awkward cute, 105

B

Babies, 3
Baby cute, 99
Baby schema, 43
Baby sparrow, 35
BABY, THE STARS SHINE BRIGHT, 46
Background of Cuteness in China, 63, 66, 89
Background/Personal Questions, 147
Baidu, 25–28
Baroque, 46
Beautiful, 33, 49, 57
Beauty, 41, 56
Bill Gaver, 25
Bobbed hair, 35
Bonsai, 44
Branding, 13
Busu-kawaii, 53

C

Carina, 60
Case Study of how Cuteness Bridges Culture
    and Technology in China, 81
Changes in the Ways to Visualize Cuteness,
    150
Child, 35
Classical Lolita, 46
Clever, 33
Color, 43
Comiket, 45, 56
Common characteristics in cute designs, 99
Common scenarios or applications in design
    where cuteness is applied, 149
Conclusion, 118
Confucian, 14
Conventions in the use of various cuteness
    features, 150
Cosplay, 56
Costume play, 56
Cultural kawaii, 42, 44, 60
Culture, 14
Culture dimensions, 14
Culture-specific elements commonly used in
    cuteness depiction, 152
Cute by appearance-identity contrast, 114
Cute by appearance–personality contrast, 112
Cute by behavior–personality contrast, 113
Cute by being scheming, 112
Cute by being smolderingly passionate, 113
Cute by Being stubbornly softhearted, 113
Cute by contrast in age, 114
Cute by contrast in appearance, 109
Cute by contrast in fame, 114
Cute by contrast in gender, 115
Cute by contrast in instrument, 110
Cute by contrast in name, 99
Cute by contrast in personality change, 111
Cute by contrast in profession, 97

© Springer International Publishing AG 2017
A. Marcus et al., *Cuteness Engineering*, Springer Series on Cultural Computing,
DOI 10.1007/978-3-319-61961-3

Cute by contrast in social status, 113
Cute by contrast in strength, 110
Cute by contrast in transformation, 111
Cute by identity–personality/behavior contrast,
      113
Cute by intangible contrast, 111
Cute by tangible contrast, 109
Cute guidelines, 28
Cute information architecture, 24
Cuteness, 155
Cuteness-age dependence, 117
Cuteness-appearance, 117
Cuteness-behavior someone, 117
Cuteness by attribute, 97
Cuteness by contrast, 109
Cuteness by contrast in multiple dimensions,
      109
Cuteness by contrast in one dimension, 111
Cuteness-context dependence, 117
Cuteness-culture dependence, 117
Cuteness-culture value, 118
Cuteness design and manufacture in China, 87
Cuteness-economic value, 118
Cuteness-education dependence, 117
Cuteness Franchise Positioning and Branding
      in China, 81
Cuteness-gender dependence, 117
Cuteness guidelines, 25
Cuteness-historical changes, 117
Cuteness in conventional culture industry, 80
Cuteness Industry in China, 78, 81, 83, 88
Cuteness in internet technology industry, 81
Cuteness IP Development in Comics and
      Animation in China, 85
Cuteness-language, 117
Cuteness marketing and Sales in China, 88
Cuteness-medium, 117
Cuteness phenomenon in design—history and
      future trend, 149
Cuteness-profession dependence, 117
Cuteness-psychological value, 118
Cuteness-related questions, 149
Cuteness-social influence, 117
Cuteness-social value, 118
Cuteness-sound, 117
Cuteness-technology orientation, 117
Cute's history, 8
Cycladic art, 1, 2

D
Data, 12
Dear Daniel, 131
Dependence of cuteness, 117
Discussion, 77

Disney, 13
Distinctive, 49
DIY Emoticon Engineering, 76
Doll, 59

E
Earcons, 25
Embarrassed, 37
Emotions Expressed in *Baozou* Emoticons, 73
Emoticons, Kaomoji, Emoji, and Stickers, 70
Ero-kawaii, 53
Eroticism, 53
Evolution of cuteness, 117
Evolution of the meaning of cuteness in
      chinese literature, 63
Evolution of the perception of cuteness in
      chinese culture, 64

F
Factors influencing cuteness interpretation, 149
Fluffy materials, 43
Fogg's persuasion theory, 22
Fox, 38
Fresh Punch, 122, 124
From Original ACG IP to User-Centric IT, 81
Fuka-fuka, 43
Funassy, 50
Fusa-fusa, 43

G
Gal, 46
Games, 55, 56
Game software, 55
Ganguro, 49
Garfield, 42
Garu, 46
Geek, 55
Gender, 3
Gender-neutral cute, 99
Gender-specific, 56
Gender-specific cute, 97
Generic kawaii, 42, 49, 60
Girls' culture, 40
Goth-Loli, 46
Gro-kawaii, 53
Grotesque, 53
Guidelines, 155

H
Harajuku, 46
Hashikoi, 33
Hello Kitty, 42, 119
Hello Kitty Boom, 130
Hello Kitty's first grand piano, 125

Hime-gal, 49
Hinamatsuri, 131
History of cuteness, 155
Honold, 1999, 14
Horror, 59
Humanoid robot, 59

I
Impact of generation on, 153
Influence of *kawaii* culture in China, 71
Influence of Moe culture in China, 63, 66
Information, 12
Information design, 11
Information visualization, 11
Intelligent, 33
Interaction, 11, 18
Internal overlapping sound, 76
International manga award, 41
Internet Meme, Rage Comics, and *Baozou*
        Comics Phenomenon in China, 69
Interpretation of cuteness in design, 149
Introduction, 147
Izakaya, 49

J
Jane Marple, 46
Japan, 33
Japanese, 42
Japanese culture, 42
Japan Expo, 41
Japonism, 39
Joshi-Kousei (JK), 49
Jui Shang-Ling, 16

K
Kahayushi, 37
Kawae import, 42
Kawai-garu, 35
Kawai-ge, 35
Kawaii, 3, 33, 133
Kawai-rashii, 35
Kawai-rashisa, 35
Kawai-sa, 35
Kewpie, 39
Kimo-kawaii, 51, 53
Kindchenschema, 43
Kireina, 33
Knowledge, 12
Koakuma-Ageha, 49
Ko-gal, 49
Konjaku-Monogatari, 37

Kumamon, 50
Kyaba-kra, 49
Kyriakoullis and Zaphiris, 15, 20

L
Length, 43
Lewis Carroll, 45
Line, 4, 5
Little Twin Stars, 122, 123
Loli, 45
Loli-con, 45
Lolita, 45, 51
Lolita complex, 45
Lolita cute, 97
Lolita fashion, 45, 46
Look-and-Feel, 24
Loose socks, 46
Lovable, 49
Love, 35
Lovely in traditional chinese culture, 64
Luminosity, 43
Lurid, Vulgar, or Anarchic Cute, 107

M
Major cute features commonly expressed in
        design, 150
Makura-(no)-Soushi, 35, 43
Mame, 44
Maneki-neko, 38
Manga, 40, 41, 55
Marilyn Monroe, 57
Market Research, 13
Maslow's theory of human motivation, 23
Matching, 49
Meaning of cuteness in the professional role of
        a designer, 149
Media elements of cuteness, 117
Meido, 55
Meido-cafés, 55
Mental models, 11, 18
Metaphors, 10, 17, 23
Mickey Mouse, 4, 42, 57, 134
Miffy, 42
Mignon, 60
MILK, 46, 133
Miniaturization, 44
Ministry of Economy, Trade and Industry
        (METI), 41
Ministry of foreign affairs of Japan, 41
MIUI, 4
Mobile persuasion design, 22

Mobile phone cases, 129
Moe, 55
Mof-mof, 43
Mona Lisa, 57
Mosa-mosa, 43
Murakami, 2

N
Naïve cute, 101
Navigation, 11, 18
Negative cute, 100, 101
Nerd, 55
Non-no, 40
Nukemeno-nai, 33

O
Orientalism, 39
Origins, 1
Orizume-bento, 44
Otaku, 55, 56
Otome-tic, 40
Out of control emotions, 73, 74
Oyaji-gal, 49

P
Pachinko, 49
Patty and Jimmy, 122, 125
Pedophilic, 55
Peko-chan, 134
Perception of cuteness among younger
      generation, 153
Personal experience with, responsibility for, or
      focus on cuteness, 148
Personality cute, 99
Personas, 20
Persuasion theory, 22
Petite Purse, 135
Pink Quilt Series, 129
Pinterest, 13
Pixar, 13
Pochette, 46
Pof-pof, 43
Pokémon, 25
Pop culture, 44
Pop idols, 55
Positive cute, 101
Pragmatic, 12
Pretty, 34
Pretty things, 37
Prof Luo, Yongxi, 17
Projection mechanism, 43
Psycho-physical kawaii, 42, 50, 60
Puri-kura, 44

R
Rei Yanagawa, 133
Retro-Futurism, 1
Rhetoric, 12
Ribbon, 40
Rikouna, 33
Robots, 24
Rococo, 46
Round shapes, 43

S
Sadism, 53
Sailor fuku, 56
Samsung, 25
Sanrio, 4, 120, 121
Saturation, 43
Scale, 20
Scarlett Johansson, 58
Sci-fi, 55
Sei-shonagon, 35
Self-satisfaction, 45
Semantic, 12
Semiotics, 10
Sensory cute, 97, 99
Sexual connotation, 45, 55
Sexy cute, 97, 115
Shape, 43
Shibuya, 46, 49
Shimotsuma Monogatari, 45
Shrinkage, 44
SIGGRAPH, 13
Siri, 25
Size, 43
Skype, 5, 6
SkypeMojis, 6
Slow-witted cute, 104
Smart, 33
Snoopy, 134
Social-psychological-economic reasons behind
      the cuteness phenomenon, 153
Sociocultural differences-related questions, 150
Socioeconomic Factors in the Rise of *Baozou*
      Emoticons in China, 71
Soft cute, 101
Space, 19
Sponge Bob, 42
Stupid cute, 104
Styles of cuteness, 93
Subculture of Diǎosī, 71
Subculture of Tǔcáo, 72
Sub-cultures, 55
Subtle or complicated emotions, 74
Suddath, 4

Suki, 55
Summary, 78, 89
Syntactic, 12

T
Taisho Roman, 39
Takarazuka, 39, 45
Taxonomy of cuteness, 9, 155
Teddy bear, 1, 127, 128
Texture, 43
The Roses of Versailles, 40
Time, 19
Tiny Chum, 127
Total impression, 41

U
Ugly, 53
Ugly cute, 103
Uncanny Valley, 59
Uniform cute, 97
Unique, 49
User-Centered Design (UCD), 9
User interface design components, 10
Use scenarios, 21
Utukushi, 37
Utukushiki-mono, 37

V
Value of cuteness, 118
Victorian, 46
Visual rock, 46
Viv.com, 25
Vivienne Westwood, 46

W
Walt Disney, 4
WeChat, 4, 5
Wisdom, 12
Wukong project, 16

X
Xiaomi, 4

Y
Yamamba, 49
Young girl, 45
Yume-kawaii, 51
Yuru-chara, 50

Z
Zadeh, 15

Printed in the United States
By Bookmasters